Michael Keeling

What is Right?

SCM PRESS LTD

334 01779 3

First published 1969
by SCM Press Ltd
56 Bloomsbury Street London WC1

Printed in Great Britain by
Billing & Sons Limited
Guildford and London

scm centrebooks

Christianity at the Centre / John Hick
Who is God? / D. W. D. Shaw
What about the Old Testament? / John Bowden
What is the New Testament? / T. G. A. Baker
What is the Church? / Victor de Waal
What is Right? / Michael Keeling
The Last Things Now / David L. Edwards
Who is Jesus Christ? / A. O. Dyson

Contents

We are grateful to abu and *The Guardian* for permission to reproduce the drawings on pages 6 and 118.

1   Making Moral Decisions

Let's start by talking about you. Every day you have to make decisions: you decide what you are going to do or not going to do in all sorts of circumstances, from crossing the road to telling the cashier she has given you too much change. You also make decisions about values: in conversation or in your own mind you say some things are 'right' and others 'wrong', some 'good' and others 'bad'. So, judging by what you do and say each day, you know what 'right' and 'wrong' mean, and 'good' and 'bad'? Fine. Now consider the following propositions:

Thou shalt do no murder. (Deuteronomy 5.17)

'You have learned that our forefathers were told, "Do not commit murder; anyone who commits murder must be brought to judgement." But what I tell you is this: anyone who nurses anger against his brother must be brought to judgement. If he abuses his brother he must answer for it to the court; if he sneers at him he will have to answer for it in the fires of hell.' (Matthew 5.21f.)

The Laws of the Realm may punish Christian men with death, for heinous and grievous offences.
It is lawful for Christian men, at the commandment of the Magistrate, to wear weapons, and serve in the wars. (*Articles of Religion of the Church of England*, 38)

It is to be hoped that the exaltation of the ideal of peace may not favour the cowardice of those who fear it may be their

7

duty to give their life for the service of their own country and of their own brothers, when these are engaged in the defence of justice and liberty, and who seek only a flight from their responsibility, from the risks that are necessarily involved in the accomplishment of great duties and generous exploits. Peace is not pacifism. It does not mask a base and slothful concept of life, but it proclaims the highest and most universal values of life, truth, justice, freedom, love. (Pope Paul VI, reported in *The Guardian* 16 December 1967)

Love for peace and commitment to justice mean for some that they must be ready to establish and defend them with force of arms, even though war is recognized as an evil. . . . For others, war and the methods of warfare may burden their consciences so heavily that the same love for peace and the same commitment to justice force them to refuse military service . . . freedom of conscience is a fundamental human right and its protection is essential to better international relations. (Reported comment by officials of the World Council of Churches on the Pope's statement, *ibid.*)

WE CHALLENGE THE CHURCH to face up to the implications of its own gospel in regard to war. The Anglican Pacifist Fellowship challenges all Christians and the Lambeth Conference 1968 in particular to show how you can support war without denying the gospel. (Advertisement in *New Christian*, 14 December 1967).

These propositions express different attitudes to killing. Deuteronomy appears to forbid killing under some circumstances ('murder'). Matthew's Gospel adds to this the thought that even ill-will against a fellow man is an immense wrong in the sight of God. *The Articles of Religion* reduce the impact of the Gospel saying by suggesting that we weigh against it the opposite idea that we have a right to defend ourselves. The Pope's statement goes further by condemning as cowards those who take the Gospel saying as an order not to kill at all. The World Council of Churches' statement tries to keep the peace by suggesting that both points of view are possible for Christians. The pacifists' advertisement states in strong terms that the only possible point of view for a Christian is that all killing is wrong. So this leaves us with two questions: Which point of view do you choose? Which is right?

These two questions are not exactly the same question. The point of view which you choose on killing or not killing is not necessarily the 'right' view in some wider sense: it may, for example, not be what God wants, or what Jesus was actually aiming to teach, or it may not be what a social scientist would say is best for the happiness of mankind. You hold it because you think it is 'right' in one of these senses, but you may be mistaken. In the quotations above, it is not possible for both Pope Paul and the Anglican Pacifist Fellowship to be right, and the statement from the two officers of the World Council of Churches admits that they do not know absolutely which point of view is right.

This doubt arises even though all the quotations are taken from within the context of Jewish and Christian teaching. If we had cast our net wider, we could have been faced with an even greater diversity of views.

We can now state two problems we have found in moral decision-making:

1. We have to choose which moral principles we are going to follow.
2. Even if we choose a moral principle from the Bible, we may be in doubt about how to apply it.

Now let's come back to you again. We will assume that on this particular moral issue of war and peace you vote with the majority of Christians in saying that there are times when it is right to fight for what you believe in.

So have a look at a recent war, the most important current example of people fighting for what they believe in: the war

9

between the government of South Vietnam and their American and other allies on one side, and the government of North Vietnam and the National Liberation Front (Vietcong) guerrilla fighters in the South (and other allies) on the other side. Is this a war in which it is right to fight?

Immediately we ask this question, it is clear that there is another question that has to be answered first, which is: 'Right for whom?'

1. From the North Vietnamese point of view the situation is that at the end of the Japanese occupation in 1945 the people of Vietnam (which they regard as a single country) established a national government under Ho Chi Minh, but in December 1946, the French (the pre-war colonial power in Vietnam) sent troops to support the return of the Emperor Bao-Dai. The Vietnamese people resisted successfully and the French suffered a major defeat at the battle of Dien Bien Phu in 1954. By an agreement at a conference in Geneva a cease-fire was arranged and the country was temporarily divided along the 17th Parallel, until free elections could be held in both halves, with the aim of reunifying the country. It was proposed to hold these elections in 1956, but the people now running the southern half of Vietnam, with American support, refused to permit them to be held. The ordinary people of the southern half of Vietnam therefore continued their struggle, through the Viet Cong, against the government imposed on them, first by the French and later by the Americans. The war is therefore seen as a civil war originating in the national uprising of 1945.

2. From the point of view of the South Vietnamese government and its allies, the revolution of 1945, however much it may have begun as a national movement, was rapidly taken over by the Communists; Communism is the enemy of democracy, and the return of the French, aided by

the Americans, was therefore an action in defence of liberty. The elections proposed for 1956 were never a genuine possibility, because experience in Europe (for example, in Czechoslovakia) had shown that once Communists got to important positions in a government, it soon became possible for them to take over the government by force. The two halves of the country are regarded as independent territories, and the war is seen as one between two sovereign states.

Both these accounts of the war are plausible. Vietnam has in the past been a single country, and both the fight against the French and the fight against the Americans had in them elements of a genuine national uprising seeking national freedom. Communism is a political system which tends not to allow freedom to political opponents and which is not acceptable to the large Catholic population of South Vietnam (approximately 800,000 refugees left their homes in the North and came to South Vietnam at the end of 1954). Against the point of view of the government of South Vietnam and their American supporters, it might be asked: how far it is a defence of liberty and democracy to impose on a country governments as undemocratic and oppressive as those of Bao-Dai and Ngo Dinh Diem have been? Against the North Vietnamese and Viet Cong view it might be asked why have the Communists found it necessary to eliminate all political opposition in the areas under their control; and why the Viet Cong find it necessary to operate by acts of terror, such as the assassination of village officials appointed by the South Vietnamese government (the South Vietnamese estimate that some 50,000 civilians have been assassinated or kidnapped by the Viet Cong since 1954)?

Our initial question was: 'Is this a war in which it was right to fight?' It is clear that the answer 'Yes' can be given by the following people:

11

1.   Those who think that Communism is so great an evil that any means should be used to overcome it ('Better dead than Red').

2.   Those who think that Communism is so great an advance for human society that any means should be used to extend it ('The East is Red').

For anyone outside these categories there is another question to explore in seeking to define our attitude to the war, which is this: 'Are the means employed in this war in any way compatible with the aims we have in mind?' Or, to put it another way: 'How many Vietnamese do we have to kill in order to save them from Communism – or from American imperialism?' The American journalist, Martha Gellhorn writes:

> US troops, upon arrival in South Vietnam, are read an indoctrination lecture of 30 mimeographed pages which is earnest, clear, and laudably humane. The following paragraphs seem best to sum up the whole:
>
> 'You and I know that we are here to *help* the people and the Government of South Vietnam. We know what our mission is: we are here to help save this valiant little country, and with it all of South-east Asia, from Communist aggression and oppression. In doing so, we will strengthen the security of the United States itself. And you and I know that we can't accomplish this mission without the support of the Vietnamese people. Everything we do to help win their support will help to shorten and win this war; and anything we do to alienate them will only weaken our effort at its most vital point. . . .
>
> 'From everything I've said, it should be plain to see that we're in a new kind of war. And the name of this new game is much, much more than just "Kill VC"(Vietcong). We've got to kill VC all right; but there's a lot more to it than that. To really and truly and finally win this war, we must help the Government of South Vietnam win the hearts and minds of the *people* of South Vietnam.'
>
> In its simplest terms, this is the American doctrine in Vietnam; and though my contacts with any US officials, civilian or

military, were brief and glancing, I had the impression that all sincerely believed it, especially the central tenet: Americans are in Vietnam to help the people and they are helping the people. (The lecture defines 'the people' as the peasants, 80 per cent of the population of the country.)[1]

The tiny children do not cry out in pain; if they make any sound it is a soft moaning; they twist their wounded bodies in silence. In the cot by the door is a child burned by napalm. He is seven years old, the size of a four-year-old of ours. His face and back and bottom and one hand were burned. A piece of something like cheesecloth covers his body; it seems that any weight would be intolerable, but so is air. His hand is burned, stretched out like a starfish; the napalmed skin on the little body looks like bloody hardened meat in a butcher's shop. ('We always get the napalm cases in batches,' the doctor had said. And there's white phosphorus too and it's worse because it goes on gnawing at flesh like rat's teeth, gnawing to the bone.) An old man, nearly blind with cataract, was tending this burned child, his grandson. The napalm bombs fell a week ago on their hamlet, he carried the child to the nearest town, and they were flown here by helicopter. The child cried with pain all that week, but today he is better, he is not crying, only shifting his body to find some way to lie that does not hurt him.

In theory, the peasants are warned of an air attack on their hamlet, by loudspeaker or leaflets 48 hours in advance, but as the military say, this is not always possible. Obviously I did not canvass the country, but I found no case in the hospitals I visited where this timetable was kept. In the areas called Free Air Strike Zones, or some such jargon, there is no warning and the people can be bombed at will day or night because the area is considered entirely held by Vietcong, and too bad for the peasants who cling to their land which is all they have ever known for generations. In this child's hamlet, the people were warned to leave by loudspeaker from the air in the night; but no one in Vietnam moves readily by night, and besides, in the dark and the haste and the fear, how could they take with them their possessions which they value fiercely just because they have so few?

That night, the boy and his grandfather, his mother and older brother got away from the hamlet with two of their four buffaloes. The buffaloes were their only capital, their fortune; without the buffaloes they could not cultivate their fields. At first light, many of the peasants crept back to the hamlet to rescue more of their livestock and household goods. The old man, too blind to go alone, took the child with him to try to find their remaining two buffaloes. But the jet fighter-bombers came at once. The two buffaloes were killed by the napalm, the old man said, and so were many of the people, and many were burned. No damages for lost property, death or wounds will be paid to these people, though the whole business of damages to civilians looks like another of the many dreams on mimeographed paper which characterize this war. But damages, if ever paid, are only paid for accidents: these people were warned, their hamlet was destroyed as an act of war.

The old man was penniless, of course; he was given 300 piastres, before coming here with the child, in part a contribution from the local authority, partly a gift from neighbours. Three hundred piastres is less than 14 shillings, less than $2.00. He now had 100 piastres left to feed himself and the child. One cannot know what will happen when that runs out; it is no one's duty to worry about him. In principle, a refugee gets 7 piastres a day from the Government for about a month; 7 piastres is a sum too small to describe in our terms, and will not buy one kilo of rice. The little boy's father had already been killed in the Vietnamese army; his mother and older brother are somewhere in a refugee camp.

Another child, also seven years old, had been burned in that same hamlet. His mother stood over his cot helplessly. The child was in acute pain; she had covered him with a light cloth and kept fanning the small body as if she could cool that wet, blood-red skin. She too had gone back to save more things from her house, cooking pots, rice, clothing. She said that the Vietcong overran their hamlet – which means that, in some force, guerrilla fighters moved into the area – in April, but were long gone; why destroy their houses and their possessions and their children now in August?[2]

Both sides in Vietnam have used a wide range of weapons, but clearly American resources are much greater than those of the other side. Martha Gellhorn quotes an estimate that

14

'it costs about $1 million per head to kill a Vietcong'.[3] Frank Harvey[4] describes some of the weapons in use: machine guns that fire 7·62 mm bullets at the rate of 6,000 per minute; the 3,000 pound 'swimming pool maker' bomb; white phosphorus bombs (Harvey saw a man in hospital who had a piece of white phosphorus in his flesh. It was still burning). He goes on:

> But the deadliest weapon of all, at least against personnel, were CBUs – cluster bomb units. One type of CBU consisted of a long canister filled with metal balls about the size of softballs. Inside each metal ball were numbers of smaller metal balls or 'Bomblets'. The CBUs were expelled over the target by compressed air. The little bomblets covered a wide swathe in a closely spaced pattern. They look like sparklers going off and were lethal to anybody within their range. Some types were fitted with delayed action fuses and went off later when people have come out thinking the area was safe. If a pilot used CBUs properly he could lawnmower for considerable distances, killing or maiming anybody on a path several hundred feet wide and many yards long.'[5]

Another technique is 'defoliation', the destruction of all vegetation in an area. It is estimated that up to 7% of all cultivable land in Vietnam has been treated in this way. It is not yet clear whether defoliation causes permanent changes in the soil structure of the affected area.

It is obviously possible to argue in favour of such a war as a means of pursuing political objectives, since the parties to the fighting in Vietnam have done just this. But if we are willing to burn seven-year-old boys in pursuit of political objectives, it is as well to be clear that this may not be a very effective method. Thich Nhat Hanh writes:

> Peasants in these villages hated both sides. The Viet Cong ordered them to dig caves as shelters from the possible bombing, while government troops warned them that if they dug caves, the Viet Cong would use them for resistance against the government. They were warned that if they refused to dig the

caves, they would suffer the consequences from the Viet Cong, and they were warned by the government that if they did dig the caves they would be beaten by the government troops. We talked with some peasants who were preparing to take some of their products to the market by boat, and when we had established confidence between ourselves I asked them the question: 'Whom would you follow: the Government of South Vietnam or the National Liberation Front?' They replied: 'We do not follow either. We follow the one who can end the war and guarantee that we can live.'[6]

Thich Nhat Hanh points out that the causes of the war lie as much in the corruption and harshness of successive governments in South Vietnam as in any plot or infiltration or attack from the north. The French established the Emperor Bao Dai in power when they came back in 1947.

The brutalities of the French continued to increase the hostility of the people. Innumerable young people left their studies in the cities to join in the resistance movement to fight against the hated invader. During this period the majority of the population continued to see the resistance as only a movement for national independence, and were unaware of the development within it of the Communist force. The so-called 'Nationalist' government of Bao Dai did carry on extensive anti-Communist propaganda, but it was unsuccessful because the people did not believe anything said either by the French or by their puppet Chief of State. The Vietnamese assumed that everything that the Bao Dai government and the French did was directed against their own interests, and the anti-Communist propaganda of these groups therefore had exactly the opposite effect from what was intended. People cannot believe in the words of those who have invaded their homelands and are engaged in shooting, destroying, burning their homes and terrorizing their fellow citizens, and this irrespective of the objective truth of what they may be saying.[7]

In 1955 the Emperor Bao Dai was overthrown by his Prime Minister Ngo Dinh Diem. Thich Nhat Hanh goes on:

But it is very doubtful that the war could have been resumed or its resumption been successful (*i.e. after the defeat of the*

16

French at Dien Bien Phu and the Geneva agreements of 1954),
if Diem had been able to create in South Vietnam a legitimately
democratic, non-Communist government with a record of
genuine social reform to its credit.

It was because Diem did not do this, but instead instituted a
bitterly repressive régime of his own, harshly liquidated the
very groups and individuals that might have helped him, and
condoned or instigated forms of social injustice, that the Viet
Cong could attract support and launch a formidable attack on
his régime.[8]

To conduct a large-scale war against the northern part of
Vietnam and against the National Liberation Front (Viet
Cong) guerrillas (or terrorists) in the southern part of the
country is possibly not the most effective response to difficulties caused by a corrupt and repressive government.
Frank Harvey points to a different kind of response in his
description of American medical aid to the civil population.
He also makes the point that, even without war, life in Vietnam is less than ideal:

I talked at length with Sgt Chuck Koscinski, who was a medic
on Donlon's A-team. He was a young redhead, and when I
first saw him he was plunging down a rope off a six-storey
wooden tower, putting on a demonstration for some visiting
brass. He did it with a little steel clip, which the rope was
threaded through, abruptly halted at the end of his plunge by
another guy with a sub-rope above him on the tower. It looked
like a thinly disguised form of suicide and Koscinski was
getting brutally jarred on each trip, but he was cheerful enough,
although a bit winded, when I met him.

He said he got into the paratroopers at age 20, won his
wings at Fort Benning, volunteered for Special Forces and
went through the 37-week course given to medical specialists.
This included work in an Army Hospital at Fort Sam Houston,
on-the-job training in a field hospital and advanced work,
including surgery, at Fort Bragg. When you finished the 37
weeks, Koscinski said, you were considerably more than an
iodine-and-stretcher man. You were called 'doctor' in Vietnam,
and were looked upon almost like a God by the natives. Kos-

17

cinski liked it so much he was getting out of the Green Berets and starting to try to work his way through college and med school with the idea of being a real doctor. He said that sick call, in his opinion, was the most effective way to win the war in Vietnam.

'Those poor little people have an average of two diseases all the time – sometimes more. Almost everybody has malaria. It's kind of the lowest common denominator. *Everybody* has stomach worms from babyhood. The skin diseases are awful. There are so many varieties it would take quite a while to list them all. Then there's typhoid, dysentery, pneumonia, flu, cholera, leprosy, and every now and then an outbreak of the plague.

'Everybody seems to be suffering from malnutrition – perhaps because the stomach worms eat up so much of what goes into their stomachs. That means that their resistance to infection and various disease germs is lower to start with. So if you have antibiotics and are able to help them eat a decent diet, and run a sick call every day, you really get to be a big man around there. You have hundreds of daily patients and sometimes you can perform what must seem to them to be a miracle. Have you ever seen a bad case of yaws?'

'No.'

'Well, it can turn a person's face into a reasonable facsimile of a piece of ground up hamburger. Penicillin happens to be a specific for it. A good course of penicillin shots and the hamburger look goes away and the kid starts to look like a human being. It can happen very fast, and it gets their attention.'

Sgt Koscinski gave his own recipe for winning the war and the peace, and from the plans subsequently issued by our high command on the conduct of the pacification of the country, they seem to be doing exactly what Chuck recommended. 'Move into a village,' he said. 'Run a daily Sick Call – real big – all day every day. Stay there. Guard the place so the VC can't come back, ever. Keep doing this in enough places and you'll win the war.'[9]

This is perhaps the place to pay tribute to Frank Harvey's very remarkable account of the war in Vietnam – compassionate, lively, committed to the American point of view and yet fully aware of the horrors of war for all concerned, it is a remarkable piece of war reporting. The only possibility it fails to take account of is that the Vietnamese – or a sufficiently large minority of them to cause difficulties – might prefer to do without American help for the sake of being free of the American presence. Thich Nhat Hanh makes precisely this claim in another passage in *Vietnam: The Lotus in the Sea of Fire:*

> All experts on guerrilla warfare point out that such warfare cannot be successful without the support of the peasants. The fact that the National Liberation Front in Vietnam gets such support is explained to Americans in terms of the terrorism inflicted by the Viet Cong on the peasants. The peasants are too frightened to do anything but support the Viet Cong, according to the informants in America. This is simply not true. The fact is that the Front has the support of a considerable number of the peasants because it has been able to persuade them that this is in fact the struggle for national independence. The spirit of patriotism among the peasants is very high. They are not informed about the history of the war, or ideological struggles; what they see is a large force of white Westerners doing their best to kill their fellow-countrymen, most of whom previously fought against the French. The peasants do not see the victims of the American military effort as dead Communists, but as dead patriots.[10]

It is not easy to say which view is correct – Sgt Koscinski's or Thich Nhat Hanh's. Probably both have some truth in them, or are true for some people. But what separates the two viewpoints more than anything else is the difference of nationality. Sgt Koscinski is an American. Nhat Hanh is a Vietnamese. Their whole lives are based on different assumptions, For an American, coming from a rich and powerful democratic society, the built-in assumption is that the western way of life, freedom of speech and association, and anti-communism are the first priorities of life. For a Vietnamese, living in a country that has been involved in war continuously for twenty-five years, the first priorities are peace and good government, and perhaps freedom from foreign (white) control; anti-communism and the western way of life tend to come lower down the list. Detached observers of other nationalities will similarly import their own national assumptions into the problem.

What you think about the war in Vietnam is for you to decide. But it is worth noticing some points about this discussions so far:

1. It is risky to make a moral decision without knowing at least some of the facts about the situation.

2. Knowing the facts is not as easy as it sounds. There have been quite a lot of quotations about Vietnam in the last few pages. How much of what is in them is fact and how much is just opinion?

3. The more we know about a situation, the more difficult it may be to come to a moral decision. If all that we knew about the war in Vietnam was that it was a war against Communism, and that Communism is a bad thing, it would be quite easy to come to a decision. If all that we knew about it was that it was a war against American imperialism, and that American imperialism is a bad thing, it would be quite easy to come to a decision. But it is not entirely clear what the war is for or against, and it is not entirely clear that either Communism or American imperialism is, for the Vietnamese, a good thing or a bad thing without any qualifications.

4. We may also note that it may be easier to make a moral decision on questions of general principles and of statistics than on the real human situation. Maybe we oppose Communism, maybe we oppose American imperialism – but either way, what precise value do we set on the life of a seven-year-old boy?

Now let us come back to you for one final question. If you have come to a decision about the war in Vietnam, and supposing that the war is still going on when you decide, what are you going to do about it? If you are a male American citizen between the ages of 19 and 26 you can either accept the draft for military service, or you can refuse (and go to prison), or you can travel to Sweden or France (if you are rich) and try to avoid it. If you live in some other country you may take part in a protest or give blood for one side or the other or talk about it in your local pub. You may feel that none of these activities in fact contributes to the ending of the war or the success of the side you favour. You may be right. So here is another difficulty about making moral decisions: whatever we decide, there may not be much that we can do about it.

NOTES

1. Martha Gellhorn, *A New Kind of War* (The Manchester Guardian and Evening News Ltd, Manchester, 1966), p. 2; originally published in *The Face of War*, Sphere Books, 1967.

2. *A New Kind of War*, pp. 5–7: Martha Gellhorn goes on to describe a child who was injured in a bus blown up by a Vietcong mine.

3. *Op. cit.*, p. 18.

4. Frank Harvey, *Air War–Vietnam* (Bantam Books, New York and London, 1967), pp. 45 ff. © 1967 by Frank Harvey. By permission of Bantam Books Ltd. All rights reserved.

5. *Op. cit.*, p. 57.

6. Thich Nhat Hanh, a Vietnamese Buddhist leader, in *Vietnam: The Lotus in the Sea of Fire* (SCM Press, London, 1967), p. 76.

7. *Op. cit.*, p. 63.

8. *Op. cit.*, pp. 64,65.

9. Harvey, *op. cit.*, pp. 48–50.

10. *Op. cit.*, pp. 78 f.

2 More Complications

Part of the difficulty of making moral decisions arises from the fact that our moral ideas are likely to be acquired in ways other than that of quiet, rational reflection. On the whole, we tend to pick them up from other people – from our parents, from our friends, from our teachers – and we pick them up as much from the way people *behave* towards us as from what they *say*. We do most of our living in groups, and therefore we have to pay attention to what other people do and say. At school we go through our time as members of an age-group, a class, a group of friends. At work we may be involved in many different groups: for example, by the kind of work we do (electrician, typist), by the place where we do it (foundry, finishing shop, sales department, north-east region), or by the status we have (apprentice, supervisor, shop steward). At home we are involved in groups again: the family (which in itself has all sorts of sub-groupings), the people we meet in our leisure time (the boys down at 'The Green Man', the Townswomen's Guild, the football crowd), and the people where we live (the neighbours, the Rate-payers' Association). We are also members of wider groups (the United Kingdom, Western Europe, 'the West').

The question is, how far do these groups influence our behaviour? Simply by the fact that they exist, they must have some influence. We have already noted in the last chapter the difference in judgment which arises from the difference between being a Vietnamese and being an American.[1] It may be, then, that our moral ideas are simply the products of these various groups: that our moral ideas are the rules which are useful for the working of these particular groups in this particular society.

Certainly, moral ideas do vary according to time and place. Western Europeans might find something odd, for example, in the sexual arrangements of other societies. Professor Morris Ginsberg, in his book *On the Diversity of Morals*, quotes from the writings of anthropologists on some African tribal societies:

'Indeed, in Bantu society,' we are told, 'physical attraction, affection and companionship usually follow quite different channels, a man desiring his wife, loving his sister and seeking companionship among his male relations and friends.' Among the Bemba, Dr Audrey Richards tells us, 'the pattern of married relations is one of economic and sex partnership, not of close companionship. In fact intimacy between husband and wife is laughed at'. So again we are apt to assume that the mental and physical well-being of children is best secured in the narrow unit of the Western family. But it may well be that children are no worse off in the extended family familiar in other societies, and, indeed, that they are better prepared to face the loss of parents or their separation, if they are equally at home in a variety of houses and are protected and educated by a large circle of relatives.[2]

Following up this last point, we might add that the Bantu or Bemba might consider the breaking-down of the family and the handing over of children to a local authority children's department, as happens not infrequently in our society, to be very odd and reprehensible (in 1965 there were over 67,000 children in care for various reasons in England and Wales).

On the other hand, Professor Ginsberg himself puts forward the view that the similarities between the moral codes of the various human societies that have been studied are more striking than the differences.[3] It appears likely that some principles of behaviour are necessary to human society wherever it is found. There is also dispute about whether human societies show 'progress' or 'development' in moral ideas. Some experts feel that they do not, but there is not a great deal of factual material to go on. What development there is seems to be in the widening of the circle of the 'neighbour' – the man to whom I have a moral responsibility.

The difficulty about the theory that our moral ideas are all relative – that they are all simply what is convenient for the group – is that this is not what we normally mean when we use words like 'ought' and 'right'. The fact that certain forms of behaviour and certain ideas about behaviour exist does not automatically establish their moral value for us. If someone says to us, 'This is what the group does', we still find it meaningful to ask, 'But is it right?' If we are to treat moral language seriously, we have to give some weight to this.

If we say something is 'right', we usually expect – or want – other people to agree with us. It is an appeal to a general standard. This does not fit in with the idea that each society makes its own rules. It fits in better with the idea that there are general ground rules for all human beings about the way to behave to one another. Again, to say something is 'right' suggests that it 'ought' to be done, and to say that it 'ought' to be done suggests that we are free to do it. If we see that someone has done something 'right', our opinion of his action will be altered if we find that he did it because he had a gun at his back, and the same sort of qualification (in the reverse direction) applies to someone who has done something 'wrong'. But if morals are simply rules for interaction in human societies, it is difficult to see where this need for moral freedom comes in. So long as the actions which are done are right objectively (that is, they produce the effects we want), why does it matter whether they are done freely or not?

The moral ideas of individuals obviously are influenced by the moral ideas and the moral behaviour of the people round about them. But individuals can go against the group moral ideas. We accused Sgt Koscinski of being influenced by the group 'America', but Martha Gellhorn is also an American and has very different ideas about the war in Vietnam. There is more to morals than social needs and social conditioning. We have to keep our own social conditioning very much in mind in sorting out our own moral ideas, but a simple social theory of morals is not easily squared with what we think we mean when we use the words 'right' and 'wrong'.

A variation on this approach to ethics that we have been discussing is the suggestion that our moral ideas have developed as part of the process of evolution. It is generally accepted that life on this planet (including human life) has 'evolved' in the sense that it has developed gradually from an originally simple form by a process of mutation and selection, some of the changes that happen spontaneously aiding the survival of a species by giving it a competitive advantage, or enabling it to adapt when the environment changes. If this process of evolution controls all life, it seems at least possible that it controls also that particular aspect of life which is the moral thinking of human beings. Indeed, it might be suggested that those similarities which Ginsberg finds in all moral codes are precisely the rules of conduct which aid the survival of the human species, and nothing more. But the proposition put forward in the theory of evolution is not 'that which is most deserving survives', but 'that which survives is the fittest (to survive)'. Or, to put it another way, 'whatever is, is fittest'. Evolutionary theory is about the process by which what *is* came to be; it is not about the value of what survives. Morals, on the other hand, is about value. On an evolutionary theory of morals, the only value involved is the survival of the human species. This is quite a substantial good, and one which, if it were thoroughly followed, might protect us from the threat of nuclear war. But even this is not a *value* for the evolutionary process – it is only a value in our own sight. There is nothing in the theory of evolution itself to lead us to suppose that the production and maintenance of the human race is an object of the process, or that the process has any object at all. If the human species destroys itself and the ants take over, this will be just another chapter in the history of natural selection. Consequently, we are entitled to hold that while evolution may account for our ability to think, it does not necessarily account for the fact that we think that it makes sense to talk about moral ideas. It is open to us to suppose that moral ideas are the product of the evolution of the species, just as it is open to us to suppose that moral ideas are the product of the group we live in, but we must be clear that to say this is to choose an option, on grounds which are by no means certain, and that there are other options open to us.

Another part of the difficulty about making moral decisions is that the way we feel about ourselves and other people depends in large measure on the sort of experiences we have had in our very early years. From birth, we first of all have to discover that there is a world outside ourselves and that other people are separate from us and not just parts of our own minds and bodies. In learning this we begin to form impressions about what the world is like and about what the people in it are like: how far it is a loving and protecting world and how far it is a cold and cruel world (for all of us it is both kinds of world); how far we can rely on it and how far it will not meet our expectations. All this comes to the very young child first of all from its mother, through her reactions to the basic actions of feeding and excreting, of touching and being touched. In the satisfaction of these needs is laid the foundation of our ability to respond to the world at all. From these early years there is a pattern of development, in which each stage has its needs – for response, for bodily pleasure, for reassurance and security; and each stage has its learning about human relationships – how to cope with mother and with father, how to cope with aggression and hatred and fear as well as with love and desire. At each stage a balance has to be struck between dependence and the need to exert our own will, our own existence in our own right, until at last, in late adolescence, we are sufficiently sure of ourselves to stand on our own feet as adult human beings.[4]

In this process, our understanding of ourselves is partly something that is fed back to us by the world around us: we can be ourselves only as much as other people will allow us and help us to be ourselves. One important way in which we need help is in learning to deal with our aggressive and destructive impulses. We need the security of loving and stable relationships in which we can show our aggression and yet be safe and not destroy the world, so learning how to contain these feelings. If this is not allowed to happen (perhaps because the parents cannot cope with these feelings themselves), the impulses do not just go away: in later life they can be turned upon some socially acceptable object (such as people of another country or colour), or turned back on ourselves in the forms of anxiety, guilt and a wish to destroy the self. We tend to blame most fiercely in others the behaviour which we subconsciously desire in ourselves, and we profess to fear on behalf of others the instincts that are powerful in us. Consequently, our moral judgments may be saying more about our own unconscious desires than about the situation we think we are discussing. The moral learning process is one in which an aggressive, anxious, loving and confused being learns from other aggressive, anxious, loving and confused beings, and consequently the moral information which we have is not altogether reliable. A substantial element in our moral 'judgments' is an emotional reaction based on our own past experiences. For this reason we have to be wary of instant moral reactions – both our own and other people's.

So now we seem to be in trouble. We cannot altogether trust our own moral reactions and yet in the end there is nothing that we can trust but our own moral reactions: whatever you do, *you* decide to do it. This is the situation in which we have to make moral judgments. There is no way out of it. There is no moral certainty in the sense in which there is scientific certainty, or in the sense in which there is mathematical or logical certainty. All there is is the need to live and a great deal of advice, often conflicting, about how to do it. Maybe you feel now that you do not really know where you are. If so, this is quite a good state to be in. It at any rate reflects the human situation. It is this possibility of making moral choices, this doubtful, painful privilege, that is one of the more important things about being a human being. Professor Antony Flew, examining the philosophical basis of moral principles, concludes as follows:

> The realistic and the courageous moral to draw from the fact that we have constantly to act without that basis for certainty which we should like to have is: not that we must delude ourselves into believing that our condition is other and better than it is; but that, having once recognized that the facts are what they are, we ought to learn to live with them with our eyes wide open.[5]

These two chapters have been concerned with the things that make moral decisions difficult, because the first point about making moral choices is that it *is* difficult. The difficulty is often concealed by the fact that we are quite good at applying the words 'right' and 'wrong', 'good' and 'bad' to situations and to people. When somebody disagrees with us we tend to think that they are wrong-headed or even evil. But what we call 'right' is what we happen to believe is right. It may not be what someone else believes is right, and it may not be right on some wider point of view. As we saw when we looked at the war in Vietnam, even going deeper into the facts of a situation does not necessarily lead us to a decision about the rights and wrongs of it that will be accepted by everybody. The question of the real basis for moral decisions remains open.

Once we are clear about the necessary standing of moral principles, we can go ahead and look at some particular moral beliefs and see how they work out. With our own moral judgments arising the way they do, it is a good idea to have *something* to check them against. The 'something' which we are going to put forward in this book is the Christian gospel, and that for a reason which may seem peculiar: that Christian morality does not bind us to rules but frees us from them, and frees us particularly from the heaviest rules of all, which are the ones that we make for ourselves. This may seem to be a large claim, and you may well reserve judgment whether it can be made good; but for a start, let us have a look at what the Christian gospel actually says about morals.

NOTES

1. See p. 19 above.
2. *Op. cit.*, pp. 108 f.
3. *Op. cit.*, pp. 110 f.

4. A simple and very readable description of the early stages of our psychological growth is *The Child, the Family and the Outside World* by D. W. Winnicott (Penguin, London, 1964).

5. A. Flew, *God and Philosophy* (Hutchinson, London, 1966), p. 183, para. 9.8.

3   The Sermon on the Mount

The New Testament does not present us with a single, clear statement of Jesus's moral teaching. It contains general moral principles and it contains some detailed instructions on particular issues, but these are scattered about in the various books according to the needs of the writers and the arguments they are pursuing. The most substantial single section is that which has come to be known as 'The Sermon on the Mount' (the Gospel according to Matthew, chapters 5, 6 and 7).

Most readers will probably know that modern study of the Bible ('modern' here meaning 'during the last 100 years or so') has shown that the material in the New Testament has come from a number of different sources. Much of it was in use as isolated stories and sayings (or as collections of stories and sayings) before it was put together in the various books that we now know. In the putting together of these books the writers (whose identities are not always clear) exercised a good deal of editorial liberty and tended to include what they thought was of use for the Church of their own day rather than what would make a documentary account of the life of Jesus. This background of the New Testament books raises two questions for us about the Sermon on the Mount:

1. Is it reasonable to treat the 'sermon' as a single unit?

2. Does the 'sermon' really represent the teaching of
   Jesus?

There is no space here to argue either of these questions,
even though they are vital to the argument which follows.
Other books in this series have dealt with the general question of the study of the Bible, and there is a vast amount of
literature available about St Matthew's Gospel and about
the Sermon on the Mount. The best that we can do here is
to repeat what is said in the most substantial of recent
studies, *The Setting of the Sermon on the Mount*, by W. D.
Davies.[1] Professor Davies accepts that Matthew's chapters
5 to 7 are made up of material drawn from several different
sources; that the needs of the Church have influenced the
form and content of the material; and that some changes
have been made because of the use of the material in church
services (for example, the additions to the Lord's Prayer:
Matthew 6.9 ff., compared with Luke 11.1 ff.). But he
asserts that Matthew did himself regard chapters 5 to 7 as a
unit.[2] He asserts also that the ethical teaching of the New
Testament does go back to Jesus himself and that 'it is a fair
assumption that we can know what the ethical teaching of
Jesus, in its main emphasis and intention, was'[3]. It is on this
basis that we shall proceed here.

With all this in mind, we may now invite the reader to
look at the Sermon for himself.

Read the Gospel according to Matthew, chapters 5, 6 and 7.

The first thing I hope this exercise will have done is to
convince you that the Sermon on the Mount does not present a simple set of rules for living, which have since been
made unnecessarily complex by people who write about
morals. On the contrary, it is itself a complex and demand-

ing exhortation to live in a way that is anything but natural or simple. It is not our business here to analyse the Sermon in detail: any modern commentary will do that.[4] Scholars differ in the way they divide the material, but one of the simplest ways is that used in the New English Bible. This breaks the Sermon up into five sections:

5.1–16: About those who will enter the kingdom of God, and an instruction to be a light to the world.

5.17–48: About the Law – we have to fulfil the Law, but to a new and higher standard.

6.1–18: About religious obligations – acts of charity, prayer and fasting.

6.19–34: About material goods and anxiety – we are to trust in God and not worry.

7: About judging and being judged – we are not to judge others, but we are to be aware that we ourselves will one day be judged.

Let us look at these sections in a little more detail.

The first (Matthew 5.1–16) consists mainly of the Beatitudes. These are statements about certain ways of living which are taken to be commendable. Those who know that they are poor are those who know that they have no claim to precedence over their fellow men, no claim to greater riches, no claim to power; they are those who know that their 'rights' are no greater than those of any other human being. Those who are sorrowful are those who know that throughout the world there is a great deal of harm done by one man to another and that there is in themselves some desire and some ability to do harm to others. Those who hunger and thirst to see right prevail are those who realize that it is not enough to avoid doing harm to others, but that there must be a deep desire, a revolutionary desire, to see that the rights of others are made good: an impatience on behalf of the wretched of the earth and on behalf of the wretched in the same street and in the same house. Those whose hearts are pure are those who have enough insight into their own motives to begin to act not for their own ends but simply because they wish others well. The peacemakers are those who are able to put into practice God's love, which does not take sides. The Beatitudes end with a recognition that this way of life will not necessarily receive approval (verses 10 to 12), but that nevertheless it is essential for the world that some people should attempt to live like this. These statements about our relationships with our fellow men are connected at every step with God, who is assumed to be more concerned about humanity than we are, so that to become more concerned is to join in his activity, not to step off on our own.

The second section (Matthew 5.17–48) emphasizes two things. First of all, that there is a Law, a right way of behaving and a wrong way of behaving: the 'Law' here, in effect, means almost everything that is said in the Old Testament ('the Law and the prophets'). Secondly, this Law is to be understood in a new way. Where the Law had once been understood to forbid murder, it must now be seen to forbid even anger against a fellow man; where once it had limited revenge to 'an eye for an eye and a tooth for a tooth', it must now be understood to forbid *any* retaliation or retribution. Where the Law had once been understood to apply only within the people of Israel, it must now be understood to include in its protection every living human being, including the unloving and the unlovable. The effect of all this is summed up in the last sentence of the section: 'You must therefore be all goodness, just as your heavenly Father is all good.'

The third section (Matthew 6.1–18) is about the relief of the poor, prayer and fasting, put under the general heading 'your religion' (*New English Bible*) or 'your righteousness' (*Revised Version*). Again the Sermon links moral activity with our relationship with God, and again it presents a heightening of the demand: relief of the poor, prayer and fasting are to be done without drawing attention to yourself; they are to be done because you want to do them, not because you want to look good.

The fourth section (Matthew 6.19–34) is on the subject of God and money. It makes three points. The first is that if we let our main interest be in material things – income, house, clothes, furniture, car – this does not in fact give satisfaction, it only leads to more anxiety. The second is that if we let our attention be divided up in this way, we are not in fact able to give much attention to God. The third is that if we give our attention to God first, our anxieties will become less and we will find that we are provided for. The emphasis of this section is that we are to be sure of God's love for us: 'You are worth more than the birds.![7] The promise is more complex than it may appear to be at first sight, because it does not mean that if we trust in God we shall have a comfortable life. That is an idea that appears in the Old Testament, for example in the Psalms:

Blessed is every one that feareth the Lord,
That walketh in his ways.
For thou shalt eat the labour of thine hands:
Happy shalt thou be, and it shall be well with thee.
Thy wife shall be as a fruitful vine, in the innermost parts of
    thine house:
Thy children like olive plants, round about thy table.
Behold, that thus shall the man be blessed
That feareth the Lord.
The Lord shall bless thee out of Zion:
And thou shalt see the good of Jerusalem all the days of thy
    life.
Yea, thou shalt see thy children's children.
Peace be upon Israel.
                         Psalm 128 (RV)

But it does not work. The point was argued out in the Book of Job and it became clear that the wicked *do* prosper and the godly *do* come into misfortune. The only answer that Job could find was to recognize that God is beyond his understanding:

> I know that thou canst do all things,
> And that no purpose of thine can be restrained.
> Who is this that hideth counsel without knowledge?
> Therefore have I uttered that which I understood not,
> Things too wonderful for me, which I knew not.
> Hear, I beseech thee, and I will speak;
> I will demand of thee, and declare thou unto me.
> I had heard of thee by the hearing of the ear;
> But now mine eye seeth thee,
> Wherefore I abhor myself, and repent
> In dust and ashes.

(Job 42.2–6)

What is being said here in the Sermon on the Mount is that those who are prepared to set their minds on God will find that in everything that happens God's love for them and their love for God will in the end be greater than their own anxieties (but not a promise that they will not have anxieties).

The fifth section (Matthew 7) deals mainly with judgment. It makes three statements about judgment. The first is that we are not to judge others. It is not our business to say how 'good' or 'bad' other people are. To do this is only to invite other people – and God – to do the same to us. The second is that we are dealing with a loving God and have only to ask to receive. The third is that if we choose to judge others and to cut ourselves off from asking of the loving God, we shall inevitably have to pay the price of this disregard. The choice is ours and the price is not unfair. Judgment is the other side of the Law, and like the Law it is presented within the setting of the love that requires us not to judge others and that says: 'Ask, and you will receive.'

Finally, the Sermon closes with a statement about the way in which the teaching of Jesus was received:

> When Jesus had finished this discourse the people were astounded at his teaching; unlike their own teachers he taught with a note of authority. (Matthew 7.28 f.)

What Jesus has to say is not something to be argued over, or laid alongside other philosophies to see which we like better. Jesus is not just speculating or putting forward his own ideas: he is telling us what we are like, what the world is like, what God is like, and we can take it or leave it.

In this connection we may notice the setting of the Sermon within the whole Gospel according to Matthew. Immediately before it begins, there is the story of Jesus calling Peter, Andrew, James and John to come and learn from him and share his activities, together with a note that he preached the Gospel of the Kingdom and cured sickness and infirmity (Matthew 4.18–25). Immediately after it ends, there come accounts of the curing of a leper, of a centurion's boy and of Peter's mother-in-law, ending with a comment from Isaiah: 'He took away our illnesses and lifted our diseases from us' (Matthew 8.1–17). It is the Jesus who heals, the Jesus who talks about God, the Jesus who demands that people believe in the Father and in himself, who gives the moral teaching of the Sermon. Both the setting of the Sermon and its contents reinforce a point which is crucial to any attempt to understand the New Testament, that the moral teaching of Jesus is bound up in the whole complex of events and ideas which lead to the idea of Jesus as in some sense 'the son of God'. If Jesus convinces us that he has something of the truth about human existence, then we have to take his teaching as we are given it, bound up with the ideas about God and about prayer and about judgment. There is no other Jesus of Nazareth. It is only by doing violence to what the documents actually say that we can get from the Sermon on the Mount a simple ethic, easy to follow, by which men may come to love each other and live in peace. In the view actually offered by Jesus, human existence is not that simple, and neither does it make sense without the idea of God.

After this brief, but, I hope, reasonably accurate analysis of the Sermon on the Mount, we may take the risk of simplifying further by suggesting that the moral teaching of Jesus can be put in just two points:

1. That morality is a matter of our attitude to other people: that it consists in an attitude of love.
2. That there is no limit to the demands that can legitimately be made upon us.

We are used to thinking of morals in terms of what we are supposed to do or not supposed to do, and consequently we may be led to think that actions are 'right' or 'wrong' in themselves, but this is not quite so. We are brought up, for example, to think that stealing is 'wrong', but if I steal a loaf of bread from the baker, it makes a difference whether I do this because I am starving or because I want to upset the baker. The act of removing the loaf is only part of a complex situation between myself and the baker and the society we live in, which includes the whole of my life (and the whole of the baker's life) and the morality of my action is related to the morality of my whole life.

If we want to make moral judgments, we have to begin by asking questions like 'What sort of life has X had?'; 'What was he trying to do?'; 'Was this his normal attitude to people?' I do not think that it is possible to make a moral judgment on a single event, without regard to the total situation, and therefore I do not think that it is possible to get very far with simple rules. This is the point that the Sermon on the Mount is making by beginning with the Beatitudes: 'How blest are those who know that they are poor; the kingdom of heaven is theirs.' The Beatitudes state that certain attitudes and ways of behaving to others are connected with the kingdom of God. It will do no harm for the moment if, instead of reading 'the kingdom of God', we read here simply 'what is right'. To know that you are poor, to be sorrowful, to be of a gentle spirit, to hunger and thirst to see right prevail, to show mercy, to be pure at heart, to be a peacemaker, to suffer persecution for the cause of right – these are 'what is right'. And at the end of the chapter, all the Beatitudes are summed up simply in the words:

> ... what I tell you is this: love your enemies and pray for your persecutors; only so can you be children of your heavenly Father ... You must therefore be all goodness, just as your heavenly Father is all good. (Matthew 5.44, 45 and 48)

It may well be that the idea of 'love' has worn thin. Although many people are agreed that we ought in theory to love our fellow men, the thought does not seem to help us much in doing it. Most people would probably be willing to settle for something rather less. Nevertheless, Jesus has given us this word. What does he mean by it?

I think it is reasonable to suggest that when Jesus demands that we should 'love' our fellow men, he is not talking about an emotional feeling: he is not likely to be asking us to produce feelings we do not have. If he is asking us to do something, it will be something that we can do. And what we can do is to begin to examine, and to exercise some control over, the attitudes we take up towards other people, exercising a little imagination to try to think how they feel and how they see things, and in particular trying to know when what we are doing hurts them.

Before 'love', before 'care', before 'concern' comes 'respect'. The first thing that we have to learn, as the foundation of all our attitudes towards people, as the foundation of all our morality, is that each person is of infinite value *as he is*. He has this value simply because he is alive, because he is a human being, because he is a person like myself, because he stands as I do in the presence of God. It does not make any difference if he is Jesus or Mahatma Gandhi or Mrs Bloggs or Adolf Hitler or Comrade Brezhnev or you or me. God loves, and that is all that needs to be said. This is the fact that overturns all ideas of social order, all ideas of justice, all ideas of personal preference.

Clearly, for some people this will be going too far. God loves, yes – but there must be some limits? There are no limits.

> ... only so can you be children of your heavenly Father, who makes his sun rise on good and bad alike, and sends the rain on the honest and the dishonest. If you love only those who love you, what reward can you expect? Surely the tax-gatherers do as much as that. And if you greet only your brothers, what is there extraordinary about that? Even the heathen do as much. (Matthew 5.45–47)

We are asked to show total compassion, total understanding, total engagement in the need of others: we are asked to give total acceptance. 'Pass no judgment, and you will not be judged' (Matthew 7.1). We are to give up the habit of making judgments about people. We are to accept, as God accepts.

Along with this overwhelming demand, there is a continuing warning against failure to face up to it.

> But what of the man who hears these words of mine and does not act upon them? He is like a man who was foolish enough to build his house on sand. The rain came down, the floods rose, the wind blew, and beat upon that house; down it fell with a great crash. (Matthew 7.26 f.)

This warning occurs too often in the New Testament to be ignored, and certainly some warning on these lines must have formed part of Jesus' own teaching. It is a warning that what he has to say is real: it is not a game and it is not a philosophical speculation; it is the truth about the way life is. If we want our lives to be acceptable to ourselves, we had better pay some attention to it, however far out it may seem to be.

If these two points – that we are to be loving and that there is no limit to the demands that can legitimately be made upon us – are a fair summary of what the Sermon on the Mount says and of what Christian ethics are about, the question that follows is whether the Christian ethic offers a way of life that anybody can or ought to take up? The answer, perhaps, is 'No'.

In the first place, this ethic is unreasonable. No sensible man would turn the other cheek, go two miles with somebody who made him go one, or love his enemies. One reason for the comparative popularity of the Ten Commandments among people who claim to be Christians is that they look, at any rate on the surface, to be much closer to what the reasonable man would expect of his moral code than does the Sermon on the Mount.

In the second place, it may be said that the Christian ethic ignores human psychology and could cause harm to anyone who tried to follow it. Sigmund Freud made this objection forcibly in his essay *Civilization and Its Discontents*.[5] He objected to the idea of universal love – love for all human beings – because he felt that love must discriminate; a love which is given to everybody is not worth much to anybody. He believed also that not all men are worthy of love and that hostility and aggression arise from a natural instinct which requires some object as an outlet. To state

Freud's views so briefly and crudely is, of course, to mis-represent them, and anyone who wants to know what Freud's arguments are must read the essay for himself. But these three points, as stated here, do roughly represent the main psychological arguments against the Christian ethic and in particular against the demand that we should love all men.

On the idea that love should not be indiscriminate, we may comment as follows. First, that as we have already pointed out, the 'love' which Jesus demands that we should apply to all men is not 'affection', but 'understanding' and 'respect'; it does not in any way conflict with the fact that we naturally feel affection, love and sexual desire towards some people more than others. Secondly, that the demand to love all men can be understood only as a demand that we should begin actively to share in the love which God already shows to them – we are not trying to stretch our own feelings to cover all mankind. Freud's remark that 'My love is something valuable to me which I ought not to throw away without reflection'[6] is interesting as an indication of his own psychological condition, but it is not entirely relevant to what Christianity asks us to do.

On the idea that not all men are worthy of my love, we may comment briefly that this is something that the Bible just contradicts. Here you have to make a choice between Freud and the Bible: this is one of the places where the Bible really does claim to be telling us something new about our-selves.

On the idea that hostility and aggression are natural to man, we need to comment at more length. According to Freud's analysis, in the essay we have mentioned and else-where, 'the instinct to aggression is an original, self-sub-sisting instinctual disposition in man.'[7] The exercise of this instinct is restricted by external authority, as the child is taught social control by its parents (and, later, teachers). In order to avoid the threats of external authority, the job of control is taken over by part of our own mental processes, which Freud calls the 'super-ego' or conscience. What the super-ego does is to turn our own aggression back upon ourselves. The super-ego works through a sense of guilt and an unacknowledged but powerful urge to self-punishment. The result is that:

> A threatened external unhappiness – loss of love and punishment on the part of the external authority – has been exchanged for a permanent internal unhappiness, for the tension of the sense of guilt.[8]

There are fairly strong grounds in the casework experience of psychoanalysts (and in common observation) for accepting this general account of the existence of an aggressive instinct and of its control by the internalization of the moral rules that are given by external authority, leading to the creation of 'guilt' and 'conscience'. Freud suggested that the tendency in this process of guilt-making is for it to go too far: in his clinical experience his patients needed to be relieved of the excessive guilt they had come to feel. Clearly, any religious or cultural demand which puts further restraint on our aggressiveness – such as the demand to love all men – increases further the burden of guilt and therefore our inner stress. Freud therefore regarded the Christian ethic as an extra and unnecessary burden. On this, two things can be said:

1. Even on Freud's own analysis, the process of guilt-making cannot be avoided, because the advance of civilization depends on the possibility of getting the aggressive instinct under control. Freud's stated intention in this essay is:

> to represent the sense of guilt as the most important problem in the development of civilization and to show that the price

43

we pay for our advance in civilization is a loss of happiness through the heightening of the sense of guilt.[9]

But he also regards the advancement of civilization as the object of human existence:

> . . . civilization is a process in the service of Eros (*sc. the life-affirming principle which opposes the death-wish or aggressive instinct*) whose purpose is to combine single human individuals, and after that families, then races, peoples and nations, into one greater unity, the unity of mankind. Why this has to happen, we do not know; the work of Eros is precisely this.[10]

2. The function of the Christian religion and of the Christian ethic, as it is overwhelmingly set out in the New Testament, is precisely to relieve us of this burden of guilt that worries Freud. Christianity is, or ought to be, not guilt-making but guilt-removing. The message is not 'be good and God will love you', but 'God loves you, therefore you are able to be good'. It is because it tells us that we are loved beyond all imagining that it can dare also to call us to love beyond our power. This is not a commandment, or even a demand, but an invitation to join in love.

There have been so many unloving actions done in the name of love, there have been so many attempts to force people to be good, that at times we lose the message of the New Testament, that love is not forced, but grows out of being loved. The psychological damage that is done when an idea of 'good behaviour' is forced on us from the outside in an unloving way is so great that we are compelled to say that a good deal of what passes for moral teaching is not moral teaching at all, but moral violence. The attempt to force other people to be good is a violation of that respect for the other which is the love that should be taught.

What, then, should we do? Well, to a much larger extent than we have yet tried, we can just leave people alone. We are entitled to protect ourselves, when the social order is really threatened, but it is really threatened much less often than we suppose. People tend to get upset when they hear talk about 'freedom' and 'love', and if we have defended the Sermon on the Mount on the one side against the charge of imposing extra guilt upon people, we have to defend it also on the other side against the charge of being too uncertain and 'permissive'. If the Christian ethic can be reduced to the sentence 'Act in love', has it not become too flexible and indefinite to be of use?

The demand to love does not stand by itself in the New Testament; in the Sermon on the Mount it is supported by a number of concrete examples of loving and of unloving behaviour, concerning anger, adultery, swearing, revenge, giving and lending, praying and saving. We are not short of indications of how this idea of love should work out in practice in the conditions of Jesus' day. It is the business of people who write or talk about morals to give us similar indications for our own day; but it is not their business to make these indications into 'rules'. An ethic that sets out a list of rules about bidden and forbidden actions tends to cut us off precisely from what we ought to be doing, which is to *listen to others to discover what we ought to do*. We cannot respect others unless we are prepared to discover them, and we cannot discover them if we come to them with rules already made, because through our rules we are judging their actions before we know anything about them. A rule is a pre-judgment and there is no room in morals for pre-judgment. What we need to discover and to say is not 'Adultery is a sin', but, 'In this situation you are hurting X, you are not being fair to Y; this is the nature of your action'. Rules reduce people to objects, whereas the business of morals is to give people their full, infinite value. The demand for precise rules may well be a sign of immaturity, and therefore of inability to undertake the life of love.

Look, for example, at the Ten Commandments. The Ten Commandments are widely regarded as a basic statement of Christian ethics. Luther and Calvin both made much of them. Despite this, even a brief examination of the actual text shows that they fall very far short of Christian moral teaching:

And God spake all these words, saying,

I am the LORD thy God, which brought thee out of the land of Egypt, out of the house of bondage.

Thou shalt have none other gods before me.

Thou shalt not make unto thee a graven image, nor the likeness of any form that is in heaven above, or that is in the earth beneath, or that is in the water under the earth: thou shalt not bow down thyself unto them, nor serve them: for I the LORD thy God am a jealous God, visiting the iniquity of the fathers upon the children, upon the third and upon the fourth generation of them that hate me; and shewing mercy unto thousands, of them that love me and keep my commandments.

Thou shalt not take the name of the LORD thy God in vain; for the LORD will not hold him guiltless that taketh his name in vain.

Remember the sabbath day, to keep it holy. Six days shalt thou labour and do all thy work: but the seventh day is a sabbath unto the LORD thy God: in it thou shalt not do any work, thou, nor thy son, nor thy daughter, thy manservant, nor thy maidservant, nor thy cattle, nor thy stranger that is within thy gates: for in six days the LORD made heaven and earth, the sea, and all that in them is, and rested the seventh day: wherefore the LORD blessed the sabbath day, and hallowed it.

Honour thy father and thy mother: that thy days may be long upon the land which the LORD thy God giveth thee.

Thou shalt do no murder.

Thou shalt not commit adultery.

Thou shalt not steal.

Thou shalt not bear false witness against thy neighbour.

Thou shalt not covet thy neighbour's house, thou shalt not covet thy neighbour's wife, nor his manservant, nor his maidservant, nor his ox, nor his ass, nor any thing that is thy neighbour's. (Exodus 20.1–17)

The Commandments begin by concentrating our attention on God. This is a good beginning. It is useful for an ethical system to take our minds off ourselves, *our* rights and *our* feelings, and to set our thinking in a wider context of the needs of others, the feelings of others, and even of the whole universe as the setting for our lives. But the God presented here has some strange characteristics. He is, for a start, the God of one particular people – Israel. He is the only God to be worshipped, but the reason given is not the sole existence of the One, but the fact that he is jealous and will punish future generations for the misbehaviour of this one and will show mercy only to those who love him. Finally, he threatens those who use his name wrongly.

The second part of the Commandments consists of practical instructions on various points of behaviour: the proclamation of a weekly holiday and six specific instructions to honour parents, not to murder, not to commit adultery, not to steal, not to give false evidence, and not to want something that belongs to someone else (including his wife). These instructions are unobjectionable in themselves; they are not always easy to keep and there are many areas of human society where their serious application by everybody concerned would substantially improve the quality of life. But the fact that stands out about them is the degree to which they fall short of the New Testament. Here is no demand that we should love those who hate us, that we should be all goodness as our Father in heaven is all good, no claim that love knows no limit to its endurance, no affirmation that we are worth more than the birds. There is no suggestion in the Commandments of the fact that we have to be loved before we can love, the basic fact of all right action. The Commandments are commendable for their brevity, but in fostering the illusion that love, mercy, humility and the thirst for righteousness can be reduced to ten simple instructions that good people observe, they may well do more harm than good. Christian writers have tried to get round the shortcomings of the Commandments by adding New Testament ideas to their exposition of them,[11] but it will not do. If the Emperor has no clothes, we must say so. The Commandments are the religious and civil code of an Old Testament people; they are not the Christian ethic. If we want any Commandments, we must be content with a simpler form: 'Love the Lord your God with all your heart, with all your soul, with all your strength, and with all your mind; and your neighbour as your self' (Luke 10.27); though the difficult part is to bring yourself to a definition of your 'neighbour'.

If there is any objective reality about moral ideas, if they in any way relate to the world we live in, there will, of course, be some regularities about the likely effects of our actions. To kill, to steal, to break a promise are actions which on any occasion are likely to hurt someone. But it is more accurate to see them as wrong when they hurt someone than as 'wrong' full stop. Simple rules such as 'stealing is wrong', or 'telling lies is wrong', may be the correct fare for children at a certain stage of moral development, but we should not wish to remain children. The reluctance to admit the flexible and even tentative nature of morality which can be seen among those who talk or write about morals arises either out of a fear of setting their own personality free or out of a fear (natural, perhaps, to specialists) that other people's moral perceptions may not be quite so fine as their own. But if we do not allow other people the opportunity to exercise their own moral perceptions we prevent their moral perceptions developing at all. I do not think that Jesus intended the Sermon on the Mount only for moral theologians.

Admittedly, if we do not work on rigid rules such as the

Ten Commandments, or the 'teaching of the Church', or whatever we want to hold on to, we are likely to be more often faced with the fact that we do not know what is right. This is inevitable. We are human beings and there *are* many times when we do not know what is right. To think you are right when you are not may be more damaging than to know when you do not know.

It is not necessary to sit around all day debating in order to come to conclusions about what is right and wrong. On the whole we seem to be able to make most of our moral decisions quickly and directly. Usually we just react according to the attitudes that we have built up. The purpose of moral studies (including this book) is to put a question mark against these attitudes; to lead us to ask ourselves: 'Where did I get that idea from?' 'Is it right?' 'Does it work?', in the hope that this questioning may lead us on to the further questions, 'What am I looking for in human relationships?', and 'What relationships are possible?' For the purpose of the New Testament is to widen – and widen very much – our ideas of who we are and what is possible to us. God does not command; God is, and what he is is love, and where his love goes is to us and to all human beings.

> Surely life is more than food, the body more than clothes. Look at the birds of the air; they do not sow and reap and store in barns, yet your heavenly Father feeds them. You are worth more than the birds! (Matthew 6.25 f.)

NOTES

1. Cambridge University Press, 1964.
2. See chapter 1 of Davies's book, especially pp. 4 f. and 13.
3. *Op. cit.*, p. 425.

4. For example, *Saint Matthew* by J. C. Fenton (Penguin, London, 1963).

5. *Complete Psychological Works*, Volume XXI (Hogarth Press, London, 1961).

6. *Op. cit.*, p. 109.

7. *Op. cit.*, p. 122.

8. *Op. cit.*, p. 128.

9. *Op. cit.*, p. 134.

10. *Op. cit.*, p. 122.

11. Luther, who is perhaps most responsible for the post-Reformation popularity of the Ten Commandments, certainly did this: see Eduard Nielsen, *The Ten Commandments in New Perspective* (SCM Press, London, 1968), Introduction.

4 Loving Yourself and Other People

Our direct relationships with other people can be roughly divided into 'functional' and 'personal'. A 'functional' relationship is one in which you do not know anything about the other person as a person – the sort of relationship that might exist between a passenger and a bus conductor or a car driver and a petrol pump attendant. A 'personal' relationship is one in which you begin to know something about the other person and to have some interest in them. Beyond these two relationships is the wider range of all the other people in the world, whom we do not know or have business with, but who nevertheless are in relation with us as fellow human beings and who from time to time enter our consciousness under one heading or another: 'the poor', 'the white races', 'the people of Vietnam'.

In the functional relationship you do not want specially to be concerned about the other as a person: you simply want to travel or to collect the fare, to buy petrol or to serve it. At one time or another, for one person or another, such relationships may be on a more personal level – particularly in small communities – but this is an addition to the relationship, not a necessary part of it. Whether or not this ought to be so is another matter. Harvey Cox, in *The Secular City*,[1] argues that these functional relationships are a necessary protection for us in modern life: we meet too many people to be able to respond to them all at a personal level:

> Urban man must distinguish carefully between his private life and his public relationships. Since he depends on such a complex net of services to maintain himself in existence in a modern city, the majority of his transactions will have to be public and will be what sociologists call functional or secondary. In most of his relationships he will be dealing with people he cannot afford to be interested in as individuals but must deal with in terms of the services they render to him and he to them. This is essential in urban life. Supermarket checkers or gas-meter readers who became enmeshed in the lives of the people they were serving would be a menace. They would soon cause a total breakdown in the essential systems of which they are integral parts. Urban life demands that we treat most of the people we meet as persons – not as things, but not as intimates either.[2]

This seems to me right, provided that for our functional relationships, as for our indirect relationships with all humanity, we keep an interest, a concern, a love that is always ready for action and that is at any given time always in action at some point where it is needed. The fact that we do not know others as persons does not mean that we have no responsibilities towards them – or they to us.

As soon as a relationship becomes in any way personal, as soon as we have some definite interest in the other, another factor enters into the situation – our sexual feelings. Our sexual instincts are involved in meetings with other people, whether they are opposite sex or the same sex, whether they are young or old, whether we feel attraction or repulsion, or whether the feeling is at too low a level for us to notice it at all. The sexual drives are a very large part of our instinctual equipment and they are an unavoidable part of the motivation of our actions.[3] Sexuality enters into most of the activities of our daily lives: a man's feelings when driving a car, the aunts and grandmothers clucking over a new baby, the crowd at a football match or the school-master training a boys' team, the worshippers in church on a Sunday morning, the crowd at a Billy Graham Crusade or the devotees of the Blessed Virgin or the Sacred Heart, two friends who enjoy one another's company, the lover and his lass or the couple with fifty years of married life together – all these are experiencing an excitement (noticed or unnoticed) which is connected at least partly with the sexual instincts. It is within this general pattern of sexual feeling that there occur the direct and recognizable experiences which we call 'love' and 'sexual desire'.

One important feature of the human sexual instinct is its diversity of objects and forms of expression. For example, every human being has some homosexual traits and inclinations:

> Psycho-analytic research is most decidedly opposed to any attempt at separating off homosexuals from the rest of mankind as a group of a special character. By studying sexual excitations other than those that are manifestly displayed, it has found that all human beings are capable of making a homosexual object-choice and have in fact made one in their unconscious. Indeed, libidinal attachments to persons of the same sex play no less a part as factors in normal mental life, and a greater part as a motive force for illness, than do similar attachments to the opposite sex.[4]

In the same way, every human being has some sado-masochistic traits and inclinations, and every human being is liable to experience some attraction to people other than the one to whom he or she has a primary loyalty. This variety of possibilities should lead us to be a little cautious in making generalizations about love and sexual behaviour. In particular, we have to be cautious about defining what is 'natural' and what is 'unnatural', because what nature does is liable to be pretty variable. On the other hand, looking at the whole human scene, what stands out is the predominance of the pattern of the attraction of male to female, the setting up of a home and the begetting of children. It seems fair to say that most people, after some initial confusion and experiment, find a partner of the opposite sex and settle down for life with them. A lot of the energy of the Christian churches has been rather misdirected to the defence of the institution of marriage, which really does not need so much attention.

The Bible certainly takes a fairly relaxed view of sex and marriage. In the stories of the Creation we find the implied teaching that our sexual drives are part of our biological inheritance, part of the way the world is made, and that they are good. The Creation stories also contain a theological statement about marriage: 'Therefore shall a man leave his father and his mother, and shall cleave unto his wife: and they shall be one flesh' (Genesis 3.24). But much of the material in the Old Testament does not live up to this idea of a lifelong one man – one woman relationship. From Abraham and his wives and concubines (including the unfortunate Hagar) to Solomon and his wives and concubines, there is a record of sexual behaviour which is rather different from the standard established later by the Christian church. There is, for example, the story of Ruth and Boaz, in which the young widow Ruth encourages Boaz to do the duty which a nearer kinsman was not willing to undertake by going in to spend the night with Boaz and asking him to take her, to which Boaz' response is: 'Blessed be thou of the Lord, my daughter: thou hast showed more kindness in the latter end than at the beginning, inasmuch as thou followest not young men, whether poor or rich' (Ruth 3.10). There is also, notably, the story of David and his several wives, including Abigail the wife of Nabal (I Samuel 25) and various concubines (II Samuel 5.13). The unfortunate friendship of David and Bathsheba, which led to the murder of Bathsheba's husband Uriah, was punished by the Lord by the death of their first child, but the second child of that union was Solomon, who was celebrated as the greatest, wisest and most just of the kings of Israel (II Samuel 11 and 12). The Old Testament clearly extends its tolerance and even approval to some sexual activities which moralists of more recent times would find it difficult to swallow. It certainly in many stories and incidental references, as also in extended passages such as The Song of Songs and some of the Psalms, celebrates the sexual relationship between man and woman (and, to some extent, between man and man – *is this is David & Jonathan* I Samuel 20) and the pleasures of family life and of children, without being closely bound to a theology of a life-long one man – one woman relationship.

In the New Testament there is a change to a more clearcut emphasis on monogamy, but even this should not be over-emphasized. The Gospels pay little attention to sexual relationships as such, and what they do say is mainly a reaffirmation of the Genesis text. Mark, for example, has only four references to sexual activities (6.17 ff., about Herod's illicit marriage to Herodias; 7.31 f., in a list of thirteen activities which 'defile' a man, only three of which are explicitly sexual; 10.1–12, where Jesus answers a question about divorce by reasserting the teaching of Genesis; and 12.18–27, where Jesus is asked a question about remarriage as a trap by the Sadducees on the subject not of sex but of resurrection). The situation is a little different with Paul and other letter writers. As leaders of the new communities of Christians they were obliged to give detailed advice about behaviour. But here also the comment about sexual matters occurs incidentally among wideranging teaching about faith and freedom. Paul, who issues

55

lists of activities that are condemned, issues also the great list of what love is like (I Corinthians 13). Furthermore, it has to be said that not all Paul's advice on sexual relationships is the law of God. Paul himself was aware of working within a tradition that goes back to Genesis (which he quotes at I Corinthians 6.16), and aware also of the distinction between what he would like people to do and what it is permissible for them to do, as also between what he teaches and what the Lord teaches (see, for example, I Corinthians 7.1–17). In all that he says he is struggling in a busy and tough life to help the Christian communities to work out the questions they press upon him; it is this same Paul who talks about God's love for us and concludes: 'With all this in mind, what are we to say? If God is on our side, who is against us?' (Romans 8.31). His teaching has to be read in the context of a biblical tradition which states firmly that God loves us and that human sexuality is part of his good gift for our enjoyment.

What these writers are doing is to take the point already made in Genesis, that 'they (two) shall be one flesh' and apply to it the immense demands made in the Sermon on the Mount, which leads them to the conclusion that the love demanded in marriage is the maximum of which we are capable. The writer to the Ephesians (who may or may not be Paul, but whose teaching is near enough to that of Paul to have his name at the head of it) gives some advice on marriage which illustrates both the strengths and weaknesses of what teaching there is in the New Testament:

Be subject to one another out of reverence for Christ.
Wives, be subject to your husbands as to the Lord; for the man is the head of the woman, just as Christ also is the head of the church. Christ is, indeed, the Saviour of the body; but just as the church is subject to Christ, so must women be to their husbands in everything.

Husbands, love your wives, as Christ also loved the church and gave himself up for it, to consecrate it, cleansing it by water and word, so that he might present the church to himself all glorious, with no stain or wrinkle or anything of the sort, but holy and without blemish. In the same way men also are bound to love their wives, as they love their own bodies. In loving his wife a man loves himself. For no one ever hated his own body: on the contrary, he provides and cares for it; and that is how Christ treats the church, because it is his body, of which we are living parts. Thus it is that (in the words of Scripture) 'a man shall leave his father and mother and shall be joined to his wife, and the two shall become a single body'. It is a great truth that is hidden here. I for my part refer it to Christ and to the church, but it applies also individually: each of you must love his wife as his very self; and the woman must see to it that she pays her husband all respect. (Ephesians 6.21–33)

Here the very high regard and care which man and woman must have for each other in marriage is linked to Christ's love for us: we belong to one another as we belong to Christ ('the church . . . is his body, of which we are living parts'). But this is mixed up with an attitude to women which seems to be very much of a particular time and place: there is a strong sense that woman is subordinate to man (in spite of the fact that in Galatians Paul comments that: 'There is no such thing as Jew and Greek, slave and freeman, male and female; for you are all one person in Christ Jesus' (3.28). It seems reasonable to conclude that at this point the far-reaching implications of our status in Christ have not been thought through because the social consensus about the position of women is much too strong for the writer to throw off. This is the kind of difficulty that a writer on morals faces in any age.

The basic statement that the New Testament makes about marriage is that in this relationship human caring for one another goes about as deep as it can go. But it is important not to take this teaching with excessive solemnity. Marriage is an arrangement between men and women in this world and marriages are made on earth rather than in heaven. There is sometimes a credibility gap between what people experience and what the Church puts forward as its teaching on marriage, and the reason may be not so much that men and women are being disobedient as that the Church is being a little high-flown about what happens in daily life. One of the points at which this may be detected is when Christian teaching about the devotion of married couples assumes that the fact of marriage means that feelings are, or ought to be, so controlled that you never feel an attraction for anybody else. One of the best of recent writers on Christian marriage, Leonard Hodgson, comments as follows:

> In no stage of its growth, so far as we have considered it, does this love demand the lifelong exclusive companionship of one man and one woman. This is the problem which faces all adherents of monogamy who hold that marriage should be based on and be the expression of love. It leads some of them to give it up, to say that things were better when marriages were arranged on other grounds and monogamous fidelity maintained by the control of feelings in accordance with God's law. As an alternative to this attempt to turn back the clock I want now to suggest that the emergence of so-called romantic love has had a valuable contribution to make to our growing understanding of what Christian marriage should be, a contribution of which we can reap the benefit if, instead of either exaggerating or belittling the element of feeling, we welcome it in such a way as to enable it to play its full part in a love which is the devotion of the whole personality.
>
> The first thing necessary is that these sexy feelings of physical attraction should be welcomed as given by God for the enrichment of human life. Next we must accept the fact that, though perhaps it may sometimes occur, it is unusual for any particular man or woman only to have them in relation to some one particular partner. In the course of a lifetime they may be the source of multiple enjoyment in many different relationships. To refuse

to enjoy them is ingratitude to God's generosity; to pretend that the enjoyment is not sexy offends against his care for truth; to think that it is something to be ashamed of is to criticize his creative wisdom.[5]

He goes on to ask how a stable marriage can be built up if this is so and suggests that sexual attraction and romantic love are not the only elements in the marriage relationship:

The deepest and most enduring ties of affection and love are forged when men and women are drawn together in the pursuit of some interest or cause which draws them out of themselves into shared devotion to a common aim. This is where the thinking mind has its part to play, asking whether this particular sexual attraction is one which has promise of coming to fruition as the enrichment of two lives joined in such pursuit of shared interests. Then the marriage is sealed with the act of will when the two vow that they will lay down their lives, each for the other and both jointly in the service of God and their fellow men.[6]

Hodgson's words could apply equally well to a homosexual relationship. A homosexual relationship is likely to be less stable than a heterosexual relationship in so far as a homosexual object-choice (in Freud's sense) may arise from a neurotic condition, a failure to mature, but it must be remembered here that neurotic conditions and failure to mature are pretty widespread weaknesses in heterosexual relationships as well. The homosexual also has no social support for his relationships in terms of understanding and in terms of the institution of marriage, with its rights and obligations – many normal marriages would flounder more than they do without this communal understanding and support. Given these conditions, it remains true that homosexuals can set up stable and humanly helpful relationships. There is no harm done to anybody in adult homosexual relationships, beyond the ordinary sort of harm that all human beings are capable of doing to one another in all relationships. Society will have to come to a time when it is able to accept these relationships openly and calmly as an ordinary part of human life. The acceptance of one another which the Gospel requires of us certainly demands this.

The major difficulty which is presented by the New Testament teaching on marriage is that of divorce. In chapter 10 of the Gospel according to Mark, Jesus clearly rules against divorce, saying, 'What God has joined together, man must not separate' (10.9), and, 'Whoever divorces his wife and marries another commits adultery against her: so too, if she divorces her husband and marries another, she commits adultery' (10.11 f.). The difficulties of interpretation in this passage are considerable,[7] but the main point at issue is quite simply this: does the fact that Jesus taught that marriage should be lifelong mean that people following the Christian ethic can never under any circumstances divorce and remarry? What we have to do here is to try to see what is really happening. What actually goes on in a marriage? Do some marriages get to a point of no return, at which the relationship is effectively ended? I would suggest that the answer is clearly 'Yes'. Is it possible for people who have been through this experience to enter into another marriage relationship, which does endure? Again the answer is clearly 'Yes'. Now it is one thing to accept a moral standard for ourselves, but it is quite another thing for us to say that it should be enforced on everybody by law. Christians believe and therefore have to teach that lifelong marriage is a good thing, but to go beyond that and say that when this has failed there cannot be a second chance is to go beyond the necessary implications of what the Bible says and to put into the approach to marriage a rigidity and impossibility of 'new creation' which does not apply to any other moral teaching. Valuable as the institution of lifelong marriage may be, there are times when its operation as a rigid institution is going to do more hurt to people than divorce and remarriage would do; when that happens, I think love demands we should do the less hurtful thing. Similarly, I think that pre-marital chastity should not be treated as a rigid law. If people feel that they are right to go further, that is their business. They may be wrong, and they may get hurt, but God puts us into the world to learn by getting hurt, and we should not try to be more clever than God. Trying to protect others by rules about chastity does not in fact save people from being unchaste, it just adds the hostility of society to the hurt that people give themselves. The real value of the institution of marriage is that it provides a serious test for the reality of a relationship. It is one thing to feel that 'No love was ever like ours'; it is quite another thing to stand before the priest or the registrar in the presence of witnesses and enter into the marriage vows. Engagement and marriage and the tradition of pre-marital chastity are social guideposts to what is likely to be the most satisfactory way of letting these relationships grow. They arise from the practical experience of human beings and, so far as Christian moral theology is concerned, they are the collective indication of what it means in practice to have respect for and to love another human being. They exist because they work and their aim is to prevent us hurting one another and to help us to love; but it does not improve on the situation to make them into rigid laws.

We undertook in the last chapter to defend the Christian ethic against the charge of giving too much freedom to people, by suggesting that if we operate rules rigidly, we cut ourselves off from understanding other people. Now we have to go rather further than this and suggest that rules cut us off also from understanding ourselves. When we have to deal with the question of sexual deviations, such as premarital unchastity, divorce or homosexuality, the application to them of the words 'wrong' or 'sinful' can prevent us from entering into the feelings and desires of the people concerned and so from understanding either why they act as they do or how much there is of their feelings and desires in ourselves. Similarly, the understanding of what is in ourselves can help us to understand the reasons for other people's behaviour and prevent us from too hastily applying moral judgments to it.

One reason why people do depart from the norm of finding a partner of the opposite sex and settling down for life is clearly the wide range of biological, instinctual possibilities that is open to us. But these possibilities exist in all of us. Those who succeed in keeping to the norms of society have shut away in their unconscious all those desires which the 'deviants' express in practice, and it is the fear of what is shut away that tends to guide the reactions of 'normal' people to what 'deviant' people do. The instinctual forces that exist within ourselves include primitive aggression and destructiveness and sexual urges towards other objects and satisfactions than those that are socially approved. Because we have learned from our earliest years that some of our desires and experiences are not socially acceptable, we are each of us in some degree afraid of what is within ourselves. Consequently we have a good deal of insecurity and frustration arising from these repressed forces that has to be worked off on some socially acceptable object. Much of the fury that is aroused by, say, pornography represents an attempt to deal with the forces within ourselves by confronting them in the shape of activities and people in the world outside us. So, for example, the judiciary may indulge in strongly emotive language about an offence: 'Judge Calls Bookseller "A Purveyor of Filth".' Some publications indulge in even stronger language: a monthly church paper carried an article on pornography containing such phrases as 'half a million items of obscenity from literary public lavatories', 'a yellowed ghoul who sells the muck' and 'this open sewer drifting through the heart of the nation'.[8] Some of the emotional reaction to people of a different colour also arises from this same mechanism of projecting our inner fears on to others – people of a different colour are useful for this purpose because they are safely differentiated from ourselves (this suggests, incidentally, that the problem of racism is not likely to be solved easily).

Paul recognizes the existence of this dark side to ourselves. In his letter to the Romans he tells of his inability to do the good which he wants to do and attributes the difficulty of right action to 'sin that has its lodging in me' (Romans 7.20). He goes on to speak of rescue by 'God alone, through Jesus Christ' (7.25), and remarks: 'The Spirit you have received is not a spirit of slavery leading you back into a life of fear, but a Spirit that makes us sons, enabling us to cry "Abba! Father!"' (8.15). This is the key to the whole situation. Because of the creation of guilt in us, we have become divided within ourselves, we are all, in some sense, 'split personalities'. The divided self which Paul describes has to be put together again, and this can be done only if we overcome our fear of the dark half of ourselves. The first move is to recognize that God is not someone who threatens us with punishment because of the dark side of ourselves; he is someone who says 'Do not be afraid of yourself'.

As long as we think that we are creatures of a lower nature, which is the flesh, and a higher nature, which is the spirit, then we shall naturally feel guilty about the exercise of the lower nature and pretend to ourselves that we must live up to what we are pleased to call our higher nature, even though this may mean living a pretence and acting a part which is not really

63

ourselves at all. It is when we see ourselves as a whole – a whole which is to be loved for its wholeness, not divided into higher and lower – that we begin to love ourselves, to love the flesh, the mind and the spirit, because the flesh, the mind and the spirit are me, and the more I know about myself, the more I respect myself. The less I feel guilty in myself, the more I shall respect, know and love others. There is no part of me for which I need feel guilty; the only guilt I need feel is when I have ceased to be myself and, at the command of someone else, be it priest, Church, politician or parent, am pretending to be what I am not, and calling it good.[9]

We are not to feel loaded with guilt when we find that we have diverse impulses and desires in us, because these are all part of ourself, and the whole person, diverse impulses and all, is loved by God. As Paul says, the Holy Spirit does not lead us back into fear, but makes us sons, able to say 'Abba! Father!' The content of the Christian good news is that the love of God for us, shown in Jesus of Nazareth, is not limited. This is, I think, an immensely hard thing to grasp the reality of. We are so held by our fears, so conditioned by the moral training we have received, to think in terms of right and wrong rather than in terms of loving and unloving, that we find it difficult to see how anyone *could* love in an unlimited, unconditioned way. But it is the message of the New Testament that God does just this.

We have been concentrating so far on personal relationships, because until we can get these right, we are not likely to be able to get anything else right. But our relationships are not confined to the people we know, or to what we have called 'functional' relationships. We are also members of a community and members of the human race; as such we are involved in relationships in which it is also possible to love or not to love. As citizens and as members of the human race we can exercise our responsibility either towards making life better for our fellows or towards making it worse. The number of problems in which we are involved is immense – racial divisions, poverty, the relationships between nations, the use and conservation of the biosphere. Each of these could do with a book to itself, but it may be enough so far as this discussion is concerned to look at one of these problems in a little detail.

Perhaps the most difficult of these problems to deal with in practice is that of poverty on a world scale, of the relationships between rich and poor nations, between the advanced industrial nations (including the Communist countries) on the one hand, and the rest of the world, 'the Third World', on the other. In 1960 the national income of Belgium, with a population of 9·2 millions was (US) $8,946,000,000 or $967 per head; that of Tanganyika in 1958, also with a population of 9·2 millions, was $498,000,000 or $55 per head.[10] There is a tendency nowadays in the West to some disenchantment with 'aid' and 'development' because of a feeling that it 'doesn't do any good'. The reason why it appears not to do any good is less clearly understood: that the trading policies of the advanced nations have largely wiped out the benefits of the aid they have given.

The odd combination of rising economic aid with restrictive import practices has been observable in a number of the industrial countries of North America and Western Europe in recent years. At the same time the underdeveloped countries have found that the purchasing power of their export products in terms of imports from the great manufacturing centres has been deteriorating seriously ever since 1951. Thus what the developed countries have been giving with one hand they have been taking away with the other.[11]

Between 1955 and 1964 the developing countries' share of world exports fell from 26% to 20%; between 1960 and 1964, the terms of trade of the countries of Asia fell by 8%.

Between 1956 and 1964 the total net flow of financial resources to the developing countries from the advanced nations (including private investment) increased from £2·3 thousand million to £2·8 thousand million – but this expansion has now come to a halt.[12] It is also true that the advanced countries have reaped a substantial long-term benefit from their commercial investments overseas. Between 1870 and 1913 Britain invested abroad £2·4 thousand million, but the net income from these investments was £4·1 thousand million; similarly, between 1950 and 1963, the USA invested $17·4 thousand million outside its own borders, but its inflow was $29·4 thousand million.[13] All this means that the talk about 'aid' to underdeveloped countries has been so far very largely bluff and that we have scarcely begun to give genuine help at any real cost to ourselves. In the Encyclical *Populorum Progressio* ('On the Development of Peoples'), Pope Paul VI put the challenge that we need:

> Let each one examine his conscience, a conscience that conveys a new message for our times. Is he prepared to support out of his own pocket works and undertakings organized in favour of the most destitute? Is he ready to pay higher taxes so that the public authorities can intensify their efforts in favour of development? Is he ready to pay a higher price for imported goods so that the producer may be more justly rewarded? Or to leave his country, if necessary and if he is young, in order to assist in this development of the young nations?[14]

The Pope also said:

> When whole populations destitute of necessities live in a state of dependence barring them from all initiative and responsibility, and all opportunity to advance culturally and share in social and political life, recourse to violence, as a means to right these wrongs to human dignity, is a grave temptation (§30).

He then drew back slightly from this brink, saying:

We know, however, that a revolutionary uprising – save where there is manifest, long-standing tyranny which would do great damage to fundamental personal rights and dangerous harm to the common good of the country – produces new injustices, throws more elements out of balance and brings on new disasters. A real evil should not be fought against at the cost of greater misery (§31).

But there are places now (particularly in South America) where Christians are asking themselves: has it come to this point? Must it come to armed violence? Perhaps it must. At any rate, no one who is prepared to join the armed forces of his own country is in a position to deny the possibility that love may resort to violence. This is a question that only those who are in the situation can answer.

Fortunately for us, not many of us are faced with the question of direct action. But the principle at stake is the same for all of us, whether we face the problems of the world as guerrillas or as taxpayers. It is the question of our attitudes to all the other human beings upon earth – of our solidarity with them or of our rejection of them. The Sermon on the Mount demands solidarity. In the crisis of May 1968, in France, there was an attack by some Frenchmen on Daniel Cohn-Bendit, the student leader, because he is a German Jew and therefore it was thought that he ought not to be mixed up in French student affairs (it was reported that some suggested that he should be sent to Auschwitz). The response of the students was to march next time with banners saying 'We Are All German Jews'. There could be no more pointed example of what the Gospel is about. This is the solidarity that we have to work out in practice. It is not sentimentality, but a moral demand: a demand that we should take account of the sort of people we are and of the sort of world we live in. It is also a choice about what sort of people we want to be, for 'The price of hating other human beings is loving oneself less'. That is not the Bible: it is Eldridge Cleaver, Minister of Information for the Black Panther Party for Self Defense in the USA, but it is what the Gospel is about.

If we cannot love ourselves, we cannot love one other; if we cannot love one other, we cannot love many others; but if we cannot love many others, we cannot love either one other or ourselves.

NOTES

1. Penguin, London 1968: see 'The Shape of the Secular City–Anonymity', pp. 52–62.

2. *Op. cit.*, p. 54.

3. See, for example, D. W. Winnicott, *The Child, the Family and the Outside World*, on the sexual relationship between mother and baby, or Freud, *Three Essays on the Theory of Sexuality*, in the *Complete Psychological Works*, Vol. VII (The Hogarth Press, London, 1953).

4. Sigmund Freud, *Three Essays on the Theory of Sexuality*, p. 144, footnote.

5. Leonard Hodgson, *Sex and Christian Freedom* (SCM Press, London, 1967), p. 65.

6. *Op. cit.*, p. 66.

7. See, for example, D. E. Nineham, *Saint Mark* (Penguin, London, 1963), pp. 259–66.

8. *National Christian News*, March, 1964.

9. Douglas Rhymes, *No New Morality* (Constable, London, 1964), pp. 18 f.

10. Sidney Bell, *Trade Blocs and Common Markets* (Constable, London, 1963), p. 167.

11. *Op. cit.*, pp. 267 f.

12. British Council of Churches, *World Poverty and British Responsibility* (SCM Press, London, 1967), pp. 19–25.

13. Paul Sweezy, 'The Future of Capitalism', in *The Dialectics of Liberation* (Penguin, London, 1968), pp. 104 f.

14. (§47; reprinted in *World Poverty and British Responsibility*.)

5 Testing for Reality

One thing all moral systems have in common is that they deal with real happenings in the world, from war in Vietnam to people getting married. So if we are to make our moral decisions properly, we have to have some facts to work on. It is no good simply saying 'This activity is right' or 'This activity is wrong' (not even if the Bible says it is right or wrong). Before we can come to a moral judgment, we have to start answering questions like 'How many people are involved in this activity?'; 'What proportion are they of the population at risk?'; 'What common factors are there among them in terms of social statistics (housing, employment, divorce rate, etc.)?'; 'What common factors are there among them in terms of psychological description?' In other words, we have to set ourselves seriously to discover what sort of people they are and why they do whatever it is that they do. Consequently, in any moral question one of our tasks is to produce a non-moral description of the situation, in order to make sure that our moral descriptions are in touch with reality. This 'testing for reality' can make quite a difference to the final moral decision.

As an example of this process, let us have a look at the question of the use of drugs, both the 'hard' drugs such as heroin and the now much talked-of 'soft' drug cannabis (marihuana, pot, hemp). Drug use first began to be recognized as a serious social problem in Britain about 1963 when groups of teenagers were getting high on 'purple hearts' and 'black bombers' (types of amphetamine pills), and public concern then led to the passing of the *Drugs (Prevention of Misuse) Act* in 1964 in an attempt to control the use of amphetamines and LSD 25. More dangerous drugs like heroin were already under legal control, but it was in this period that their use also began to rise. The figures for known addicts from 1959 to 1966 are as follows:

Total Addicts to	1959	1960	1961	1962	1963	1964	1965	1966
Dangerous drugs	454	437	470	532	635	753	927	1,139
Heroin	68	94	132	175	237	342	521	749
Heroin, under 20	nil	1	2	3	17	40	134	200 approx.
Heroin, aged 20–34	35	52	87	126	162	219	310	?[1]

The public reaction to this sudden rise in drug use had two curious features. The first was that it was very much stronger than the public reaction to other social problems, such as alcoholism and road deaths. The comparison with alcoholism, which is also a form of drug use, is particularly instructive. Commenting on the figures for drug addiction given above, the report *Drug Dependence in Britain* says:

> These figures show only the known addicts. As there are many who are not recorded, it is estimated that there are probably at least 2,000 in Britain today, of whom 1,600 are in London. The figures show that the number of known heroin addicts has more than doubled in the last 3 years. An American research institute estimates that there may be 11,000 by 1972, if recent trends continue. Whilst the figures are small by comparison with 75,000 in New York, it is clear that the trends are alarming.[2]

Alarming they may well be, but even the figure for New York pales a little in comparison with the estimated 500,000 alcoholics in this country. Writing in *The Guardian* on 5 July 1967, Harold Jackson said:

> The danger area lies in those who stumble through their lives without actually revealing that they suffer the progressive and debilitating disease of alcoholism. The social pressures against making their plight known are enormous and yet, as Dr Chalke (*secretary to the Medical Council on Alcoholism*) observes, they present an infinitely greater problem than the drug addicts who are currently causing such concern.

On the figures for numbers of alcoholics, Jackson observed:

> There are no precise figures about the numbers of alcoholics but informed estimates put the nation-wide total at as many as half a million. Of those something like 70,000 are in what is termed the 'final stages of the disease'. Research into the problems created by them is still in its swaddling clothes and the usual desperate search for funds is still going on.[3]

In one week, selected at random, 13 to 18 November 1967, *The Guardian* carried the following items:

Nov. 13   CENTRAL BUREAU TO FIGHT DRUG ADDICTION URGED (p. 3)

Nov. 14   POP MUSICIAN ON DRUG CHARGES (p. 1)
SEVEN ON DRUGS CHARGES (p. 3)
THE DREAM WORLD HORROR 'MAY LIMIT USE OF LSD' (p. 3)
DRUGS MAIN TREATMENT FOR ANXIETY PATIENTS (p. 5)

Nov. 15   NO DRUGS CASE AGAINST WOMAN IN RHODES (p. 9)

Nov. 16   IS MR. ROBINSON'S GUIDANCE HOPELESSLY MISGUIDED? (A 'GUARDIAN' ENQUIRY INTO TREATMENT OF DRUG ADDICTS) (p. 4)
REMANDED POP ORGANIST HAS SECOND SURETY (p. 5)
RULES FOR ADDICTS REISSUED (p. 16)

Nov. 17   LSD CAUSE OF BABY'S DEFORMITY (p. 22)

Nov. 18   ALARM OVER BRITISH YOUTH ON DRUGS IN ISTANBUL (p. 3).

In the same week *The Guardian* carried one reference to alcoholism (Nov. 17, p. 4), though to be fair it should be added that there were also two items about the 'Breathalyser' tests and one item about the ending of prohibition in West Bengal. It may be suggested that this news balance is more likely to arise from editorial policy and public demand than from a shortage in that week of incidents of disorderly behaviour under the influence of alcohol in the country as a whole.

The second curious feature of the public reaction to the rise in drug use is that it was primarily a reaction to the rise in drug use by the young, and it ignored almost completely the massive use of amphetamines and barbiturates on prescription by other sectors of the population. The report *Drug Dependence in Britain* shows in the table we have just quoted a rise in heroin users under the age of 20 from nil in 1959 to 134 in 1965, but it also shows a rise for users between the ages of 20 and 34 from 35 to 310 in the same period, and gives the figures for users of other drugs as follows:

> 3 million prescriptions for amphetamines and 6 million for barbiturates were signed in 6 months of 1966. 506 adults used barbiturate as a suicide agent in 1964. At least 400,000 are on a slower road to suicide through addiction to a drug called alcohol.[4]

A survey published by the Automobile Association magazine *Drive* showed that 130 out of 945 (14%) drivers of private cars and commercial vehicles interviewed had taken pills or medicine of some description within the previous 24 hours. *Drive* comments that 14% of the total driver population would be 2,000,000 people and that most of the commonly prescribed drugs can have side effects that affect driving ability.[5]

Nevertheless, in the news media drug use is still seen as mainly a phenomenon of the young. To prove this statement would really require thorough research into all the news media for the years from 1964 to the present day, but for the purposes of the argument here we may concentrate on one of the focal points in the recent history of 'the drug menace' – the prosecution of two members of 'The Rolling Stones' group in the summer of 1967. The case arose when the police raided a house in Sussex. At the subsequent trial, Keith Richard, the occupier of the house, was found guilty of permitting the premises to be used for the purpose of smoking cannabis resin: he was sentenced to one year's imprisonment and ordered to pay £500 costs. Mick Jagger was found guilty of being in possession of 4 tablets containing amphetamine sulphate and methyl amphetamine hydrochloride: he was sentenced to 3 months' imprisonment and ordered to pay £100 costs. Another member of the party, Robert Hugh Fraser, pleaded guilty to being in possession of 24 tablets of heroin: he was sentenced to 6 months imprisonment and ordered to pay £200 costs.

The judge who conducted the trial, Judge Block, clearly felt some sense of dissociation from the defendants, and expected the jury to feel the same, for he said to the jury, according to *The Guardian*:[6] 'I ask you to put out of your minds entirely any prejudice you may feel about the manner in which he (Richard) dresses.' *The Guardian* reported:

> When Richard went into the witness box yesterday he was wearing a black four-button Regency-style 'Mod' suit, trimmed with black braid, and a white dog-collared shirt with a black stitch pattern. On his right hand he had a large silver ring with a red stone.

(As I write, I have before me a photograph in today's newspaper of two elderly gentlemen. One is wearing white artificial hair which comes down at the front to below his shoulders, a white jabot and a long black coat trimmed with gold. The other is wearing an early nineteenth-century mili-

73

tary uniform, with a hat trimmed with large feathers and a coloured sash worn diagonally across the breast. They are, respectively, the Speaker of the Northern Ireland Senate and the Governor of Northern Ireland.)

On appeal, Keith Richard had his conviction quashed and his sentence set aside; Mick Jagger had his sentence changed to a conditional discharge for 12 months; Robert Fraser's appeal was dismissed. *The Guardian*[7] reported the Lord Chief Justice's reasons for the decisions on Keith Richard and Mick Jagger as follows:

> The court, he said, was quite satisfied that it would be unsafe to allow Richard's conviction to stand. What had finally led him and his colleagues, Lord Justice Winn and Mr Justice Cusack, to quash the conviction was that even if he was right about admitting the evidence about the girl, the trial judge should have warned the jury that there was only 'purely tenuous' evidence which could persuade them that the girl had smoked cannabis resin, and that Richard knew about it.
>
> When it came to dealing with Jagger, Lord Parker explained that he had read the case with great care because it had received 'considerable interest'. The case against Jagger had been proved, but in his favour there were only four tablets, he was taking the pills with the full knowledge of his doctor, he had not been over-indulging, and there was nothing at all about peddling.

In the light of this comment the original sentence takes some explaining. It cannot stand even on the morally dubious ground of the need for an 'exemplary' sentence, since Lord Parker also believes in exemplary sentencing, saying to Mick Jagger:

> When one is dealing with somebody who has great responsibilities as you have – because, whether you like it or not, you are an idol of a large number of young people in this country – you have grave responsibilities, and accordingly if you do come for punishment it is only natural that those responsibilities will carry a higher penalty.

Judge Block's original sentences seem to have been something of an over-reaction – a point which is emphasized by a comment he is reported to have made at a dinner some months later:

> We did our best, I and my fellow magistrates, to cut these Stones down to size, but alas, it was not to be, because the Court of Criminal Appeal let them roll free.[8]

In an article in *New Society*, 'The Respectable Stones?',[9] commenting on the case, Paul Barker noted that there were some grounds for the unfavourable reaction of the older generation (and of some members of the younger generation) towards the group:

> Their career since they first topped the hit parade in July 1964 is strewn with headlines like
>
> 17 HOTELS BAN THE ROLLING STONES
>
> ROLLING STONES IN US FLAG INCIDENT
>
> THE STONES BARRED BY TOWN
>
> Fans Hosed
>
> ANGRY FANS RIOT AT 'STONES' SHOW
>
> This was part of their build-up – just as the Beatles (who are older) moved via a different build-up towards their MBE's.

But he also suggested that:

> The Stones cussedness is not all press-image. Partly, I suspect, it is what many people's behaviour would look like if it were watched as closely as this. As Keith Richard said at the trial, 'There was a complete lack of privacy from 1963 onwards'. To quote Jagger again: 'We don't go out of our way to be nice to people.'

In any case, the reaction of the respectable side of society could be equally violent; Mr Barker quotes an anonymous Glasgow magistrate who is said to have asked a boy up before him: 'What's the attraction for you with morons like that? They wear hair down to their shoulders, wear filthy clothes, act like clowns and you buy a ticket to see animals like that.'

The *Sunday Telegraph*, in an article by T. E. Utley headed 'No Martyrdom for the Stones',[10] written after the first trial and before the appeal, carried the following remarks:

> One crucial fact about the case, however, ought not to be allowed to escape the attention either of mourning teenagers or their too triumphant elders. The object of those sentences was not to censure pop culture, but to give firm and clear proof of society's determination to put down drug-taking by the young.

The leader column on the same page ('Drugs Dilemma') began:

> Pending appeal, opinion about sentences passed on two of the Rolling Stones pop group and their companion, found guilty of drug charges, must be restrained. It can be more out-spoken on mounting confusion in the public mind as to what our social, moral and legal attitudes ought to be towards the different drugs we now loosely lump together as 'dangerous'. Without more authoritative guidance, there is real danger that the Law will look ridiculous, and growing defiance, founded on ignorance, will aggravate what has become among the young not a cult but an epidemic.

This brief dip into the Rolling Stones case and some of the reactions to it suggests three comments. The first is that there is a tendency, as we have already suggested, to make drug use a matter of the young (Mick Jagger had 4 amphetamine tablets; the article in *Drive* from which we have already quoted states that in England and Wales there were 16,100,000 NHS *prescriptions* – not tablets – for barbiturates and 14,700,000 for tranquillizers issued in 1967). The second is that there seems to be a tendency towards rather hysterical exaggeration of the amount of drug use among the young ('not a cult but an epidemic'). The third is that there occasionally comes to the surface in these reactions an underlying hostility and aggressiveness towards the young and towards their way of life. It is possible that the adult population, and particularly those who inhabit the power structures, have taken drug use by young people as an area of activity which can act as a focus for the differences between the generations – which are particularly acute in a time of rapid change – so that emphasis on drug use among the young now justifies the older generation in their general attitude to the activities of the young. At the same time, by presenting drug use as primarily an activity of the young, the older generation defines an area of activity dissociated from itself and from the main structures of society, into which its own anxieties and aggressive impulses may safely be directed. The existence of anxiety and aggression in the adult human being is one of the most fundamental factors – if not *the* fundamental factor – that we have to take into account in forming moral judgments about the events of everyday life. There is no space in this book to go into this point fully, though we shall return to it in the next chapter, but the reader may be referred to the works of Freud, Jung, Adler and their followers, and particularly to Erich Fromm.[11] As an illustration of the violence of feeling that results from the pressures in the adult personality and of the way in which this violence may be directed specifically towards the young, consider this quotation from the 'Miscellany' column of *The Guardian*:[12]

CAMPUS CRUSADER

Ah, the tolerant wonders of American education. Quote, following one New York City College student demonstration: 'The first thing I'd do with those kids is pour a bottle of castor oil down each of their throats, just like Mussolini did, to clean out their insides. Then I'd throw each of them into a vat of lye and get their outsides clean. Then I'd give each of them a haircut and a shave and then I might talk to them.' (The speaker? Not some Officer McLuskey or Governor Reagan: merely Eugene Avalone, City College Dean of Campus Development and Planning.)

There is, in short, at least some case for suspecting that the public reaction to drug use contains elements other than a calm and rational consideration of the addictive properties of chemical substances; that it is in fact a vehicle by which certain fears and animosities of one sector of the population are projected on to another sector. This means that it is very difficult to arrive at a rational idea of what drugs do and of what we should do about them. Moral judgment is confused before we start. 'Testing for reality' means being aware of this situation and taking it into account whenever we talk about drugs, even when we are dealing with the medical evidence – for doctors as much as anyone else can come to irrational judgments. So, having considered the atmosphere in which we have to operate, let us now look at what evidence there is about what drugs actually *do*.

An article in the *Sunday Telegraph*, portentously labelled *Cannabis: Danger on World Scale*, by Sir Harry Greenfield ('President, International Narcotics Control Board'), after listing various governments and government officials as being 'resolutely alert' to, 'acutely sensitive' to and 'viewing with considerable anxiety' the dangers and effects of cannabis, concludedlamely:

> Considering that cannabis has been known to man throughout recorded history, the literature on this subject is relatively scanty. It is already possible to assess the harm to society where abuse of cannabis leads to impairment of the individual's social and economic functions. Much more needs to be known of the long-term physical effect on the user.[13]

The article shows no sign of any awareness whatever of the conditions under which people become drug users (apart from a somewhat wild reference to the industrialization of India). So much for the International Narcotics Control Board. In real life, the factors which lead any one person to use drugs are complex. From the small amount of work that has been done on the subject, it seems safe to say that the problem of drug users lies not so much in the addictive properties of the hard drugs as in the psychological and social factors which predispose people to use them.[14] One detailed study is that made by Chein, Gerard, Lee and Rosenfeld of teenage drug users in three boroughs of New York City (Manhattan, the Bronx and Brooklyn), published under the title *Narcotics, Delinquency and Social Policy*.[15]

In looking at the results of this study it should be borne in mind that the factors which affect drug use in New York City are not necessarily those which affect it in England or elsewhere (for example, English towns do not have anything precisely equivalent to the large racial groupings of Negroes and of Puerto Ricans in New York); nevertheless, the evidence of this study seems to establish as a general proposition the claim that, so far as 'hard' drugs are concerned, drug use is primarily a response to social and psychological pressures which the individual finds intolerable, and that while there would be no drug use problem if drugs were not available, there would then be other problems which would serve the same function. The 'drug problem' is a problem of people whose personalities and circumstances dispose them to use drugs. Consequently, as a moral problem, drug use raises questions of personality development, of family relationships and of the social and economic conditions provided by society for its citizens, rather than the simpler and more attractive questions of 'rebel youth',

'moral degeneracy', 'dope fiends' and 'evil "pushers" '
which show up in popular discussions.

Chein and his colleagues note the irrationality of response to the whole question of drug use to which we have referred above:

> We did, however, eventually reach conclusions – in briefest version, that the problem of addiction is commonly viewed in the most violently distorted perspective and that the efforts of society to cope with the problem are models of irrationality.[16]

They make a distinction between *physiological dependence*, *personal involvement* (the setting up of a life-style as 'a drug addict'), and *craving* (the demand for gratification that can be subjectively experienced as something special),[17] and point out that since various combinations of these factors are possible, it is over-simplified to refer just to 'an addict', or to a drug as 'addictive', without further definition:

> ... heroin has no universal addictive impact, and certainly not if taken in intervals of more than a day. Furthermore, there is some evidence that many youths go on using heroin on a more-or-less irregular basis – e.g., week-end and party use – for several years and eventually stop altogether. In our study of heroin use in gangs, we found that, of the eighty current heroin-users, less than half were using daily or more often and that fourteen boys who had used heroin in the past had stopped completely.[18]

The authors state in their Introduction:

> We started with the common belief that prolonged use of narcotic drugs is intrinsically devastating to the human being, physically and psychically, and it was not until we set to work to prepare a true–false test on information about narcotics that it was brought home to us how completely without any scientific foundation and contrary to fact such a belief is.[19]

They state one of their final conclusions briefly as follows:

The evidence indicates that all addicts suffer from deep-rooted, major personality disorders. Although psychiatric diagnoses are apt to vary, a particular set of symptoms seems to be common to most juvenile addicts. They are not able to enter prolonged, close, friendly relations with either peers or adults; they have difficulties in assuming a masculine role; they are frequently overcome by a sense of futility, expectation of failure, and general depression; they are easily frustrated and made anxious; and they find both frustration and anxiety intolerable. To such individuals, heroin is functional; it offers relief from strain, and it makes it easy for them to deny and to avoid facing their deep-seated personal problems. Contrary to common belief, the drug does not contribute rich positive pleasures; it merely offers relief from misery.[20]

Some of the other points they make are that drug use is associated with poverty;[21] that drug use is not a cause of delinquency – it may lead to an increase in crimes aimed at getting money for drugs, but it is also associated with a *decrease* in crimes such as rape, assault, automobile theft and disorderly conduct;[22] and that the majority of juvenile regular users are not initiated into drug use by an adult pusher: 'Most take their first dose of heroin, free, in the company of one or more boys of their own age.'[23] Within this general picture there is no clear evidence that marijuana 'leads on' to heroin use in a causative sense. In interviews conducted by the authors in 1953, eighty-three out of ninety-six users of heroin had smoked marijuana, forty of them regularly, before they began using heroin; but in another study, of street gangs, 'there were many juvenile heroin-users not known to have started with marijuana'.[24] Marijuana is in much more common use than heroin and 15% of the controls (non-users) had had some experience with marijuana.[25] In view of the evidence about the main causative factors of heroin use given by Chein and his colleagues, the most that can be said is that in a drug-using sub-culture, marijuana use is a common preliminary *for those who are going to get on to heroin anyway* (being in this respect on a level with alcohol and nicotine). The discussion of the evidence in *Cannabis*[26] by Sir Aubrey Lewis seems to me to give too little consideration to the sociological factors noted by Chein which tend in American conditions to make the cannabis-using milieu and the heroin-using milieu overlap, without necessarily implying a causative connection.

These quotations from Chein necessarily omit the statistical and clinical evidence and the careful qualifications in the body of the book, but they do provide an indication of the central form of the problem – that it is not primarily a problem of the effects of narcotic drugs. It is worth drawing attention to three points:

1. The connection of drug-use in New York with socioeconomic deprivation. The areas with the highest rates of drug use are also those with the highest percentages (70% or more) of Negroes and Puerto Ricans (economically the most deprived social groups); they are also the areas with the highest proportions of families on very low incomes.[27] This is not a simple correlation between poverty and drug use; the authors interpret it:

> not in terms of the direct impact of poverty on the youth, but in those of the community atmosphere. The youngsters react to the values and practices they experience and not simply to the material deprivations from which they suffer. The most vulnerable are, at least among the whites and the Puerto Ricans, not those from the poorest families in their neighbourhoods.[28]

This the authors think may be because there is more real possibility of movement away from these neighbourhoods for whites and Puerto Ricans and that therefore when a slightly better off family in these racial groups stays in a deteriorated neighbourhood, this may be an indication that there are other things wrong with the family.

2. The fact that adolescence is a time of considerable stress, in which revolt against adult control has to be balanced against a need for security to be provided by the adult world while the adolescent deals with his internal conflicts:

> The teen-ager, therefore, counts on the adult to keep him within bounds and on a safe course, and the very controls against which he so vigorously rebels are essential to his sense of security. His burgeoning impulses impel him to defy restraints, but they also threaten the integrity of his selfhood, for the very vigor and inchoateness of his impulsive life threaten to engulf him and sweep him into depths in which, for all he knows to the contrary, he may never be able to resume control.
>
> Moreover, with the imminence of the time when he must stand on his own, the issues of the *self* – who and what am I? where do I belong? what shall I be? what goals, what restrictions, what behavior am I to accept as appropriate for me and what am I to reject as not fitting? – become extraordinarily acute. The adolescent is impelled to define a distinctive identity for himself and is, at the same time, full of too many conflicting possibilities to be able to commit himself to one *identity*. He needs the shelter and restraint of an understanding adult to give him the freedom to experiment with personal identities and the assurance that no one act or series of acts necessarily represents the final commitment. To the observing adult, he may seem immersed in a struggle to seize (prematurely, from the adult's viewpoint) the requisites of the adult status, but, consciously or unconsciously, he dreads being abandoned to adulthood.[29]

3. The fact that drug users tend to come from homes where they have been either over-indulged or frustrated:

> The addict fairly typically grows up in a home where he is an *object* to be manipulated and controlled, to be ignored except when he gets in the way of the grown-ups, or to serve as a target for poorly repressed impulses. The control (*i.e.*

non-addict) typically grows up in a home where he is another *person*, to be responded to with the give and take that his *person*ality implies, with respect for and adaptation to his needs and with appreciation for what he, as an individual, has to offer. The difference even emerges in the manifestations of religion in the family life. In the one case, it is formalistic, ritualistic, empty of genuine feeling, essentially manipulative or conciliatory of supernatural powers for the advancement of one's own ends; in the second, however prominent actual ritual may be, it makes for a sense of oneness and lends grace to the home.[30]

So we come back to the question of testing for reality. We have tried to establish, so far as is possible with current knowledge, what are the realities of drug use in our society. We have found first of all that there is on the one hand a not very large proportion of the teenage population using amphetamines or cannabis illegally, and a smaller proportion still using heroin (legally or illegally), and on the other hand a rather large proportion of the adult population using amphetamines and barbiturates legally on prescription, but not cannabis, and a very small proportion of adults (roughly equivalent to the proportion of teenagers) using heroin (legally or illegally). We have also found a very widespread use of alcohol among the general population, with serious effects on a minority. In terms of *number of users + effects of drug* we would expect the order of public concern with drug use to run: 1. alcohol; 2. amphetamines, barbiturates, etc., on prescription; 3. cannabis and amphetamines not on prescription; 4. heroin and LSD. A brief dip into the press has suggested that in practice this order is reversed and that public concern operates in inverse ratio to the reality of danger.

We have found, secondly, that the causes of drug use are very far removed from the public picture of them. It is not the case that:

the only factor relevant to the spread of drug addiction is the prevalence of inducements to try the drugs and that, once one has partaken of them, there is, subject only to continuation of access, a physiologically inevitable course to addiction.[81]

On the contrary, the use of hard drugs is primarily a matter of vulnerable individuals, and of family and social circumstances that tend towards vulnerability. Here again the public reaction is at the maximum remove from the facts, the debate being conducted almost entirely in terms of 'trafficking' and the supply of drugs.

The emphasis in public policy on the 'control' of drugs is almost certainly misguided. So far as hard drugs are concerned, the present British policy of maintaining registered heroin addicts on regular doses, while providing supportive services and opportunities of withdrawal, seems reasonable enough and it is doubtful whether the further attention to control and punishment for illegal possession of heroin adds anything useful to it. It increases the work of the police, it raises the black market price of heroin and makes the smuggling of it more profitable than it would otherwise be, but it has yet to be shown that it seriously affects the supply to those who want it. The sudden rise in heroin addicts in Britain does not seem to have been a question of availability – there was no obvious and sudden failure of the measures of control in the period from 1959 onwards. What seems more likely is that there was a rise in demand (for reasons that would repay close investigation) which the market met.

So far as cannabis is concerned, the grounds for the present laws against its use are certainly not very good. On any impartial assessment cannabis is not a more harmful drug than alcohol and may in fact be less harmful.[32] It has already been decided, beyond any present question, that society can tolerate the use of a drug of the potency of alcohol on a massive scale – Laurie quotes £20,000,000 as the current annual expenditure on *advertising* alcohol in Britain.[33] The refusal to legalize cannabis seems to be a discrimination against one sector of the population on account of the fantasies of another sector and this is not a negligible matter, because it means that an unjust price is being paid by some members of society in terms of legal action, fines and imprisonments and damage to careers. Michael Schofield points out that in 1967:

> Of the 2,419 people who were convicted of possessing less than 30 grams of cannabis, 373 (15%) were imprisoned. This table also shows that 1,857 persons without previous convictions for any type of offence were convicted of possessing less than 30 grams of cannabis; 237 (13%) of these first offenders were sent to prison – 119 of them were aged 25 or less.[34]

On the evidence it presents, the Wootton Committee could well have gone beyond its recommendations to reduce the penalties for the possession of cannabis and recommended that they be removed altogether. The answer 'Then let them keep off cannabis' is not sufficient if there are no objective grounds for discriminating against cannabis. For those who find it difficult to believe that so many people, including the government and the medical profession, can be so wrong about cannabis, there is some instructive material in Chein on earlier parallel attitudes to coffee and tobacco (at one time tobacco use was punishable by death in some countries and in others coffee 'pushers' were severely punished).[35]

From the point of view of the Christian ethic this excursion into the realities of the drug situation has been important for several reasons:

1. It has raised a question which might otherwise have been overlooked of *justice* towards drug users (particularly users of cannabis) and towards young drug users as a sector

of the whole drug using population. Anyone who is taking the Sermon on the Mount seriously ought to care at least as much about justice as about drug use.

2. It has suggested that public concern about drug use may be a cover for public refusal to be concerned about other questions of love and of personal relationships in families, in schools, in the churches, in working life and in the agencies of government; questions which in the end may be much more important and potentially more damaging than the use of narcotics. If we have begun to see that public concern about drug use, far from being an expression of moral indignation, may be a fundamentally escapist and immoral exercise, then we have begun to make the sort of readjustment that can be demanded when we test for reality and begin to apply the Christian ethic seriously.

3. It has suggested that a certain amount of violence and hostility underlies and to that extent invalidates some common attitudes and common moral judgments.

4. It has emphasized that at the bottom of all moral problems is the question of recognizing, or failing to recognize, the value of the individual human being, of treating people, in Chein's words, as objects or as persons – a process in which religion can work on either side.

5. It has demonstrated again that moral realities tend to be complex rather than simple, and that simple moral conclusions rarely stand up to the facts.

This is a cautionary tale that needs to be borne in mind whenever we find ourselves making moral judgements about the things that happen in society.

NOTES

1. *Drug Dependence in Britain* (Church Information Office), London, 1967, p. 6.
2. *Op. cit.*, p. 7.

3. 'Nation's alcoholism problem "worse than drugs" ', p. 4.

4. *Op. cit.*, p. 6.

5. 'The Drugged Driver', *Drive*, New Year 1969, pp. 30–35.

6. 30 June, 1967, p. 3.

7. 1 August, 1967, p. 1.

8. *West Sussex Gazette*, 1 November 1967, quoted in *New Christian*, 11 January 1968, p. 8.

9. 6 July 1967, pp. 6–8.

10. 2 July 1967, p. 12.

11. Erich Fromm, *The Fear of Freedom* (Routledge, London, 1960).

12. 22 November 1967, p. 8.

13. 26 January 1969, p. 16.

14. As the Report by the Advisory Committee on Drug Dependence, *Cannabis* (HMSO 1969), shows, cannabis is in a different category in this respect; see pp. 14–16.

15. *Narcotics, Delinquency and Social Policy*, Tavistock Publications (London, 1964).

16. *Op. cit.*, p. 7.

17. *Op. cit.*, pp. 22–29.

18. *Op. cit.*, p. 159.

19. *Op. cit.*, p. 6.

20. *Op. cit.*, p. 14.

21. *Op. cit.*, pp. 10 and 47–77.

22. *Op. cit.*, p. 11 and pp. 166 f.

23. *Op. cit.*, p. 12.

24. *Op. cit.*, p. 149.

25. *Op. cit.*, p. 149.

26. *Cannabis*, pp. 53 f.

27. *Narcotics, Delinquency and Social Policy*, pp. 59 ff.

28. *Op. cit.*, p. 127.

29. *Op. cit.*, pp. 130 f.

30. *Op. cit.*, p. 297.

31. In the words of Chein and his colleagues, *op. cit.*, p. 5.

32. See *Cannabis*, pp. 5 to 14; Chein, *op. cit.*, chapter XIV; also Peter Laurie, *Drugs* (Penguin, London, 1964), chapter 1.

33. Laurie, *op. cit.*, p. 15.

34. *Cannabis*, p. 36, para. 1.

35. *Narcotics, Delinquency and Social Policy*, pp. 337–41.

6 The Moral Guardians

What is the present moral state of our society? In particular, how tolerant is it? What you think about that depends, of course, on where you start from. Quite a number of people think that society ought not to be very tolerant at all. A phrase that is sometimes used to describe our current moral condition in Britain is 'the permissive society'. This is the sort of phrase that is so vague as to be almost meaningless (who is permitting what to whom, when?), but it is in sufficiently common use to be worth some attention. Generally it is used to refer to the fact that the law has in recent years been altered to make divorce rather easier (with further alterations proposed), to make certain homosexual acts no longer an offence, to recognize wider grounds for the termination of pregnancy, to remove the powers of the Lord Chamberlain over stage productions, to introduce the defence of literary merit in prosecutions for obscenity and to abolish capital punishment (for five years); it is also used to refer to a more general impression that social conventions have changed concerning discussion of sexual relationships, the expression of sexual interest in public, the use of obscenity and nudity on the stage and in the other arts, the way the young dress and the use of drugs.

It has to be admitted that many people are very worried about all this. From what is said in the press and on television, and from private conversations, I would guess that many of those who are in some particular sense responsible for the maintenance of the established social order (*Drug Dependence in Britain* lists 'Doctors, teachers, social workers, youth leaders, clergy, police and parents', to which we might add 'members of Parliament, lawyers, magistrates, judges and officers of the armed services') believe that British society, and probably western society in general, is less 'moral' than it was, say, thirty or fifty years ago. Some of those mentioned would associate this with the decline in religious observance to be seen over the same period. How far is this a correct impression?

It is very difficult to check morality by statistics. In the first place, there is, as we have already noted, a lack of agreement about precisely what is 'right' (a difficulty that is increased if we realize that Britain is, and always has been, a plural society, with people professing many religions, and many people professing none). In the second place, statistics do not always tell a clear story. For example, the proportion of illegitimate live births to all live births is rising if you take the figures for the last ten years, but if you compare the last ten years with the decade 1851–60, the current figure is lower than that of a century ago. It might then be said that the reason for the difference is not better morals in this decade than 100 years ago, but better contraception. This is probably true but, on the other hand, the increase within the present decade corresponds to a decline in the number of teenage brides who were pregnant on their wedding day, and is therefore presumably connected with a decline in 'shotgun' marriages, which may be a moral gain. Beyond these statistical considerations there are questions of different attitudes in different social classes, of the effect of changes in the environment (a look at the social conditions of the poorest classes in Victorian England might lead one to wonder why there were ever any legitimate births at all), and of the precise psychological motivation which leads women to put themselves at risk to 'unwanted' pregnancy (the very low involvement of women in criminal activity may suggest that pregnancy is the chosen form of rebellion against society, as delinquency is for boys). The statistics are complex enough in themselves, but once we begin to look at such underlying factors we may reasonably conclude that there is very little hope of arriving at an objective judgment about contemporary moral trends. The effect of this conclusion is to reinforce the teaching of the New Testament – that we should be wary about making moral judgments.

It is very difficult to check the relationship between religious observance and moral attitudes, because the crude statistical averages of opinion polls do not tell us much about the very complex relationship between belief and action in the individual person. Nevertheless, two points seem reasonably certain. The first is that the decline in religious practice which has been observed in Britain in the last 100 years (that is, since the religious census of 1851) is the product of a large number of factors acting together: the effect of exposure to the scientific attitude through mass education, the work of Darwin, Marx and Freud, the experiences of the two world wars, the increased mobility of the population, changes in working hours (especially shift and Sunday working), and changes in the availability of entertainment have all combined with some aspects of the activities, attitudes and teaching of the churches themselves to reduce the number of people who 'go to church' (how far beliefs have changed as well is a different question). The second point that we can be fairly certain about is that the moral openness or permissiveness which is evidenced by the changes in the law that we listed at the beginning of this chapter is also the product of a large number of factors acting together, many of them being the same factors that have changed religious practice, such as the scientific attitude, increased psychological understanding and sociological change. It is quite inadequate to say that there has been a change in moral attitudes simply *because* there has been a change in religious belief or practice. To say this is to refuse to try to understand the world in which we live and the highly complex relationships between personality and environment, and between belief and practice.

The widespread use of the phrase 'the permissive society' does indicate that many people have a sense that things are changing more widely than just the changes in the law. Without the benefit of what we might call 'hard' evidence, let us too venture into the realm of impressions. The main change seems to have been in the general direction of openness, in particular of sexual openness, with a recognition of the fact that both masculine and feminine elements exist in each of us and can be expressed, so that the line between the sexes has become a little less clear-cut than it has been in the past. There is, at least in some quarters, a greater tolerance, a greater willingness to let each do 'his own thing', coupled with an increase in political awareness, in concern for the quality of life. Now these are all changes that connect closely with what the Gospel is saying to us. The Gospel demands openness, willingness to trust, and freedom. It demands that we should be willing to let each do his own thing. It demands that we should be more honest about our own feelings and our own needs. It demands that we should try to express towards each other the immense love that God has for each of us. Since the moral changes which are taking place are changes in the direction which is required by the Gospel, it does not seem to me to matter whether they are taking place because people are following the Gospel or because they are following something else –

scientific humanism, or Freudian psychology, or existentialist philosophy, or Franz Fanon or Herbert Marcuse. Far from joining in an outcry against 'the permissive society', I think that Christians ought to welcome the development of a better way of treating each other.

The question is not really, 'Is society too permissive?' but 'Is society permissive enough?' Does society yet come anywhere near giving us enough room for moral growth and enough respect as persons? The phrase 'the permissive society' contains the answer within itself. The word 'permissive' suggests that there is a right inherent in society, or in the leading individuals in society, to exercise control over us and that they are failing in this duty, inasmuch as certain activities are 'permitted' which ought not to be 'permitted'. It suggests that the controls have slipped. So long as this suggestion can be made – and taken – seriously we have not begun to realize what the right relationship between ourselves and society is. It is not the business of society to control us. It is the business of society only to provide the basic civil liberties within which we can make our own moral decisions and discover our own possibilities for moral growth. Beyond this we might wish society (which is only ourselves acting as a group) to act in love towards its members, but this is an immensely difficult requirement for any society and I suspect that it will be expressed chiefly – in any age – in the degree to which society is willing to leave us alone. The main difficulty which stands in the way of this is the desire each of us has to exercise control over others. This desire springs, as we have already suggested in earlier chapters, from the fears within ourselves and from the fact that we tend to project on to others our own feelings and fears. The exercising of control over others is an extension of the need which we feel to control ourselves. We have already noted how this operates on a large scale in relation to drug use by the young, but it extends much more widely than this. The fear of 'the permissive society', which is so widely expressed by those who are responsible for the maintenance of the established social order, is, I think, primarily a defence mechanism against their own inner urges and fears.

These are strong words. Can they be justified? Let us first of all restate what the Bible says about relationships between man and man and between man and God:

> God is love; he who dwells in love is dwelling in God, and God in him. This is for us the perfection of love, to have confidence on the day of judgment, and this we can have, because even in this world we are as he is. There is no room for fear in love; perfect love banishes fear. For fear brings with it the pains of judgment, and anyone who is afraid has not attained to love in its perfection. We love because he loved us first. But if a man says, 'I love God', while hating his brother, he is a liar. If he does not love the brother whom he has seen, it cannot be that he loves God whom he has not seen. And indeed this command comes to us from Christ himself: that he who loves God must also love his brother. (The First Letter of John 4.16–21)

Love comes from God; if we understand this love there is no place for fear; because he loves us, we must love others also in the same way. The key phrase here is 'perfect love banishes fear'. We need have no fear of God's attitude to us on the day of judgment (in itself a sufficiently remarkable statement); we need have no fear of others in our loving of them. This is the standard that we are to apply to our society as it actually is.

The suggestion we have made is that our society, as represented by many of its leading members and by many of its lesser members, does not express the love and freedom that we find in the Gospel, but that on the contrary it acts, or tries to act, in a way which is controlling and fearful;

that in the name of 'good' and of 'order' society offers at times behaviour which is really a form of moral violence. We do not need to look very far for examples of this. Some recent statements from British public life will be enough to show whether or not there is any truth in the charge.

Let us present first of all Her Majesty's Secretary for Education and Science. Mr Edward Short has been faced with the problem of student rebellion. The rebellion is not peculiar to England: it is to be found in America, in France, in Germany and in every western nation (it is also to be found in other parts of the world, but under different conditions and for rather different reasons). The students are up in arms about two things. The first cause of rebellion is a general discontent about the activities of society at large: in America about the division between black and white, about the war in Vietnam, about the attitudes of police and politicians, about poverty; in England the discontent is to some extent a reflection of the American experience, a feeling that our society is going the same way and is involved in the same compromises and the same half-truths. The second cause of rebellion is a series of specific claims concerning the universities themselves, and particularly a claim by the students for a greater share in the running of them. There is a feeling that the universities have become too big, too anonymous, that their approach to education has taken too little notice of the changes in education at other levels and of the changes in society around them and therefore of the changes in the needs of students also. Students, having come to the universities to be taught to think clearly, have begun to think about their own lives and the societies they live in, and do not altogether like what they have found. Naturally, in a situation like this, those most eager for change and those who desire the deepest changes have come to the fore. Mr Short's most noticeable response to this situation was a speech in the House of Commons in January 1969. He said:

> 'The ills of society are not the fault of the vice-chancellors or the directors of their schools or colleges. It is monstrous to disrupt the life of a college, university or school because of Vietnam, Nigeria, or race, or because you are opposed to capitalism.
> This small corps is not interested in redressing grievances either in school or in society. They are out to destroy and disrupt.'

They were a tiny handful of people, fewer than 30. Four were from the United States – subsidized to the extent of between £1,000 and £2,000 for their one year masters' degree course by the British taxpayer.

> 'They are not Socialists, nor even respectable Marxists. They are a new brand of anarchist. Some are Maoists and some of a new brand X of revolutionaries for whom as yet there is no name.
> They are wreckers. They are there to disrupt society. Their weapons are lies, misrepresentation, defamation, character assassination, intimidation, and more recently physical violence.
> In the short term they are causing harm to the educational chances of the vast majority of students who are just as idealistic and decent as ever they were. The time has come for everybody with influence to exert it to stop this squalid nonsense.
> If apprentices behaved like this they would be out on their necks – it is high time that some of these thugs should be out on their neck.'[1]

Mr Short may well be right about the aims of some students, though his description does not correspond to what some other observers saw of the students at the London School of Economics and elsewhere.[2] But the point of note in his speech is the violence of the attack which he makes, under the cover of parliamentary privilege, on people he does not name. For a Minister to use language as violent as this as the response of the Government to demands which, however brashly expressed, may well be legitimate criticisms of society, is an example precisely of the quality of violence and the disregard of persons in society that the students are protesting about. Mr Short did not offer physical violence, but I think that he offered moral violence. There are other points in Mr Short's speech which are of interest: the difference between apprentices and students (apprentices have been known to go on strike, but of course for money, which is permissible in a property-oriented society); the question whether the fact that a student has come from overseas reduces his civil rights and stature as a human being; the difference between respectable and unrespectable (or did Mr Short mean respectful?) revolutionaries – but we have not space to go into these.

Let us turn to another example, this time at local government level. The *Daily Mail* on 5 July 1968 (p. 3), reported an attempt by Haringey Council to use security men with guard dogs at Hornsey College of Art to keep out their rebellious students. We might suppose that when guard dogs are the response of organized society to demands for an improvement in human relationships in education (which is one of the factors in the students' demand for more participation), then organized society has got into pretty low moral water. The failure of Haringey Council to formulate at that point any human response to its students is as clear an example as one could ask for of the rightness of students to be in revolt. Fortunately, dogs are rather better at relationships than are local councils: the students fed the dogs and the dogs were withdrawn.

Coming a little further down the ladder of authority in education, it was reported on the same page of the *Daily Mail* that the Headmaster of a Lincolnshire secondary school sent two fifteen-year-old boys home from school 'with orders to get a haircut – two weeks before they leave school for good', because 'their sideboards are too long'. Now I do not know enough about the people involved to take sides in this particular dispute, but I quote it because it is the sort of dispute that is reported from time to time from different schools, and although it is a minor incident, it does raise the question whether the attempt by headmasters to dictate in matters of personal appearance to boys of fifteen is not in fact an invasion of privacy and of human rights that again has an element of moral violence in it. To be ordered to get your hair cut, at that age, because someone else does not like the length of it, may not be the best sort of moral instruction for the young. Concern for people is not limited to particular ages, groups or particular issues: it is indivisible.

Let us turn now to another member of the British Government, from the Ministry of Defence. Mr Gerald Reynolds was questioned in the House of Commons about the release of boy soldiers from their engagements. For boys who join the armed forces at the age of 15 have to sign, at 15, for a period of service not only until they are 18, but also for several years as adults after their 18th birthday. It is accepted on all sides that a boy at 15 is unlikely to know what sort of career he will want, and indeed what sort of a person he is going to be, at the age of 18 and thereafter. It is also known that many boys join the services at 15 because they are unhappy at home and have little idea of what adult service life will be like. There are consequently strong humanitarian arguments for allowing those who join the services at 15 to choose again at 18 whether to continue or whether to leave. Mr Reynolds admitted in the House that these arguments are strong:

Mr Reynolds said he shared the desire of the Latey Committee and MPs from all parties not to bind young men too tightly to long engagements undertaken in their immaturity. The Government departments concerned would continue studies to see whether a satisfactory solution could be found.

Nevertheless, he said that boys would not be given the right to be released from their service at 18, because the services would by then have invested time in them and might run short of qualified men if they left:

> If this recommendation [for a right to automatic release] were accepted, the forces would be unable to replace their losses and the ability of the Government to carry out its responsibilities for defence would be seriously impaired, he said.
> 'The forces are unique and cannot be compared with civil industry which is able to bear the easy circulation of labour. It takes a long time to make an efficient serviceman.'[8]

On the other hand, Mr Reynolds has 'repeatedly claimed that only a tiny fraction of the boy entrants want to be released'.[4] In other words, Mr Reynolds may be taken to be saying that the Government is not as much worried about the real needs of its younger citizens, about the lives and happiness of boys not yet full grown, as it is about its economic investment in their training. We may ask ourselves, what sort of an army is this – and what is the moral quality of a society that allows itself to be defended on these terms?

Thirdly, among members of the Government, there is the case of the Home Secretary, who rejected the report of the Home Office Advisory Committee on Drug Dependence (*Cannabis*) which suggested that the penalties for the possession or use of cannabis should be reduced (not abolished).

> In a hard-hitting Commons speech, the Home Secretary yesterday called on Britain to combat 'the so-called permissive society'.

He was speaking during a debate on the Wootton Report, which advocated reduced maximum penalties for the possession or use of the drug cannabis.

Mr Callaghan said it came as a surprise, if not a shock, to most people when 'that notorious advertisement' appeared in *The Times* in 1967, to find that there was a lobby in this country in favour of legalizing cannabis.

His reading of the Wootton Report was that the committee had been over-influenced by the existence of this lobby. At the end, those in favour of legalizing 'pot' were pushing the rest back all the time, so that eventually they got these rather remarkable conclusions that it would be wrong to legalize it, but the penalties should be reduced.

'I feel that the existence of this lobby is something which the House and public opinion should be ready to combat, as I am. It is another aspect of the so-called permissive society.

I am glad that my decision (against the proposals) has enabled the House to call a halt in the advancing tide of so-called permissiveness. I regard it as one of the most unlikeable words invented in recent years. If only we could regard ourselves as the compassionate society, the unselfish society, or the responsible society, I would be prouder of 1969.'[5]

To reject the report of a committee of this stature on the grounds that it has been influenced by a pro-pot 'lobby' is a fairly substantial insult and one which does not argue for a high degree of rationality on the part of the Minister. The language about 'the advancing tide of so-called permissiveness' and the lack of any detailed refutation of the arguments of the committee on a scale equal to that of the original report might suggest to an observer that the Minister and many of the members of the House of Commons were giving vent to an emotional reaction not closely connected with the facts. *The Guardian* reported of the Minister's original statement on the subject:

Few Government decisions have been greeted with such enthusiasm by MPs of all parties. Mr Callaghan was loudly cheered as he added that it would be 'sheer masochism' to make it easier for people to introduce another social evil into the country.[6]

We have already suggested in chapter 5 some reasons why these emotions should be so strong. If the argument there is sound, we may perhaps understand this attitude of the Home Secretary and of the House as another example of that violence towards other people which arises more from the needs and frustrations of those who exhibit it than from the real doings of the people towards whom it is directed. It may be noted that the desire of Mr Callaghan and of the members of the House of Commons to protect people does not extend as far as not wishing to fine them, or to put them into prison, for the possession of what are at the most mildly harmful drugs not greatly different from those indulged in by Members and Ministers themselves, such as alcohol. Mr Callaghan, like his colleague Mr Reynolds at the Ministry of Defence, would also presumably be willing to send these same people to kill or be killed should the need arise. This selective concern and selective righteousness, coupled with the rather suspect emotion which goes with it, make it rather difficult to take very seriously the claims of those who inhabit the organized power structures to be in any but the most minimal sense moral guardians.

We must not lose sight in all this of the fact that the Members of Parliament (or any other democratic ruling body) represent and focus the moral sense of many other members of the community and that their moral judgments and moral actions are therefore the judgments and actions of most of us, writ large. Mr Callaghan in his reaction to the report on cannabis reflected a fair body of opinion. As Ian Aitken commented in *The Guardian*:

To be fair, Mr Callaghan's critics recognize that his attitude to the Wootton Report is likely to be popular in the country

101

at large. Few people imagine that being kind to hippies, yippies and other assorted long-hairs is a vote-catching activity.[7]

Similarly, when Mr Fred Lee, Chancellor of the Duchy of Lancaster and Minister with special responsibility for the North, expressed concern at the opening of a new approved school unit for girls in his constituency in the words 'Why should girls of this character, who have been rejected by society everywhere else, be allowed to come to Newton-le-Willows?', he was expressing a complaint which is heard whenever a new institution for offenders is proposed anywhere (to give credit where credit is due, the chairman of the local council promptly dissociated himself and his council from Mr Lee's remarks, and other residents wrote in to say how much the work of the existing unit for boys is appreciated in the district). Again, public choices in matters of expenditure reflect public choices in matters of morals. The public mood a few years ago demanded the spending of a good deal of money on making British prisons 'more secure'. One of the results of this choice can be seen in the following report (which incidentally casts more doubts on Parliament's – and our – concern for the young):

PLIGHT OF 500 BOYS IN GAOL HORRIFIES J.P.S

Crowded 'Scrubs'

Mr Callaghan, the Home Secretary, is being pressed to take immediate action to relieve the plight of nearly 500 boys aged between 15 and 21 at Wormwood Scrubs prison in West London.

A group of magistrates visited the prison to see conditions. They have reported that the boys are locked up in a wing which is filthy, insanitary, corroded with dust, disgustingly fitted out and overcrowded to bursting point.

Only 80 of the boys are given any work to do, it was claimed. The rest are kept in their cells all day except for two hours exercise [*this point was later denied by the Home Office*].

The magistrates came from the Wimbledon Bench, headed by their chairman, Mr S. W. Billingham. Some were so horrified by what they saw that they now refuse to send a boy to Borstal because they know he will go to Wormwood Scrubs to be allocated.

The wing is described by the Home Office as an allocation centre where boys are supposed to spend only three weeks before going on to a Borstal. Because Borstals are full some are spending months and the major portion of their time in the prison.

Nevertheless, there is little chance of a break-out. Wormwood Scrubs is a maximum security prison, with floodlit walls watched by television cameras and all the devices recommended by the Mountbatten Inquiry on Prison Security.

A Home Office spokesman confirmed to me yesterday that 478 boys are being kept in a wing intended to accommodate a maximum of 318.

In recent months Lord Gardiner, the Lord Chancellor, has drawn the Home Office's attention to the danger of conditions becoming overcrowded in the boys' wing. He was asked to do so by Mr F. H. Cassels, chairman of South-west London Quarter Sessions.

I have seen a boy carried out of the dock at Bow Street screaming: 'Don't take me back to the Scrubs.'

The Wimbledon magistrates' plea has been placed before the Home Secretary by Sir Cyril Black, Conservative MP for Wimbledon. Other points made by the magistrates are these:

1. The sewage installation is inadequate and on some mornings overflows on the upper floors and runs over the balcony on to the lower floors. The only preventive action taken has been to roof over with plastic material a part of the ground floor where the food is served.

2. The state of repair of the cells is disgusting and the bunks are a disgrace.

3. The whole boys' wing is dilapidated and does not appear to have been decorated in any way for many years.

4. Boys are allowed only five minutes for a bath because there is insufficient bathing accommodation.[9]

To this an article in *The Economist* added two points: that the magistrates should have seen the wing two and a half years ago, when it contained 700 boys, not 500, and that:

> Public outcry over escaping prisoners in 1966, even though there were only an average number and even though all but five (out of 79) were recaptured (and one of these five is now said to have been murdered), stung the Government into spending £2½ million on implementing the Mountbatten proposals for improving security.[10]

This was a community choice in the allocation of resources. I think that it illustrates something of the fear-ridden, punitive and irrational instinct which underlies some of our most important public decisions, and the way in which concern for persons takes second place.

Yet another example can be found in the treatment of gipsies and other travellers by local authorities:

> Behind a barricade of earth 3 ft high and 20 ft deep seven Irish travelling families waited sullenly yesterday for the next move in Walsall Borough Council's attempt to find a final solution to its gipsy problem.
>
> The only way into the shabby car park where the gipsies are camping in the Digbeth shopping centre is across a mound of mud. The Council has sealed off all the entrances – as it has done to those of the other 120–150 vacant sites in Walsall – in a 'scorched earth' policy which is costing it between £2,000 and £3,000.
>
> Only three miles away, the urban district of Aldridge has spent £200 on providing an official site for six Irish gipsy families. And Aldridge has made itself worth a national study as one of the few local authorities in Britain to find a peaceful answer to its gipsy troubles.[11]

We may note here again the extent to which a public body will go in spending money on violent action as opposed to alternatives which are cheaper and more humane but which are *emotionally* unacceptable.

Why is there this preference for violent expression and sometimes for violent action? One reason is the connection of violence with sexual feelings. This is obvious in the cruder forms of violence. The two following quotations are from eye-witness accounts of police brutality in France during the crisis of May 1968:

'A young couple took us in. We were seven. The CRS beat on the door – "Open up, or we'll break down the door." They went downstairs again, to find an officer, and the officer gave the order to throw paving stones through the windows, and then grenades. The couple and three comrades went down and the girl in her nightshirt found herself completely naked and they dragged her into the street, doing I don't know what to her, but wanting to make her go across Paris all stripped. They pushed their sticks between her legs "for a joke".'

'About 11 the van arrived at Beaujon. We were driven into a small room where an officer took our personal effects. About 15 "Guardians of the Peace" formed an alley in front of the immense waiting room. On the way there, the prisoners were beaten savagely. I protested to the officer against this behaviour, pointing out again that most of us were innocent. I was seized and in my turn suffered truncheon blows, fist, knee, foot, over all my body, in particular my head, stomach and testicles.'[13]

Significantly, a report in *The Guardian* on the progress of the war in Vietnam contained this paragraph:

At the other end of the US armoury of course is the ultimate in bunker clearing, the B-52 Stratofortress: a single mission of six bombers can deliver hundreds of 750lb and 500lb bombs sufficient to saturate an area a little less than that of Hyde Park.

'We call it an orgasm,' one American intelligence officer told me, 'because it blots out everything.'[13]

In Wright's next article, when a crew reported that a target had been hit, their colonel was said to be so excited 'he almost had an orgasm'.

To put it briefly, violence can be a substitute for orgasm. It is a release of sexual feeling which has been frustrated from finding expression in other channels. The ultimate in violence, so far as peace-time society is concerned, is the death penalty, which is the extreme act of this form of sexual expression. There are no rational arguments in favour of the death penalty: it is quite clearly *not* a more effective deterrent than any other.[14] The European Committee on Crime Problems came to the conclusion that, so far as the evidence goes, as a general principle in the treatment of crime humanitarian systems of treatment are no less effective in reducing the probability of recidivism than severe forms of punishment.[15] Nevertheless, at a meeting of women Conservatives on 18 February 1969, Mr Edward Heath, Leader of the party, made a bid to collect any votes there may be in a move towards reintroducing capital punishment in Britain, saying that abolition will

again be reviewed by Parliament next year – thanks to a Conservative amendment for which I voted when Mr Sydney Silverman's abolition Bill was introduced in 1965.[16]

A Police Federation spokesman, anxious to keep the issue non-political, was quick to point out that the amendment had not been Conservative policy, but a private member's move. In view of the evidence noted above, it may not be altogether unreasonable to suggest that at least some of those involved in demanding a return of capital punishment may do so from feelings that have their origin in the sexual instinct.

These examples are illustrations of the way in which the deep forces within us may influence and even govern what we would wish to consider for ourselves and to present to others as rational approaches to life. The fear of the presentation of the human body and of what is called 'obscenity' comes under this heading. What are we to make, for example, of a court case in which a nun gave evidence that her pupils had to pass a shop window and saw 'a fairly large picture of a woman naked from the waist up, which was causing the children to whisper among themselves'?[17] Or of a vicar who was reported to have objected when his eleven-year-old son got in to see the film 'Barbarella', which had an 'X' certificate, because the film included a scene of Jane Fonda floating naked in free fall – one might think that few sights could be more beneficial for an eleven-year-old boy! Why should there be this fear of children seeing the human body? After all, they have bodies themselves, they will certainly one day enter into adult sexuality, and meanwhile they have – and enjoy – their own sexual feelings at their own level. The attempt to 'protect' them from the sight of the adult human body is likely to convey to them chiefly the existence of an adult conviction that there is something about the body which is shameful. This indeed is a conviction that is held by adults, and it may even be aesthetically true of some bodies, but sexually it is not true of any body. This fear of the human body (which is, after all, one of the more important items in God's creation) may well be a good deal more damaging than the desire on the part of other parties unduly to exhibit it. In the creation story it is not the fact that Adam and Eve are naked that is an offence, but the fact that they suddenly become afraid and ashamed of being naked – this is the 'knowledge' which separates them from God. It is really, I think, the adults who feel themselves to be in need of protection. In the case for the prosecution for obscenity of the book *Last Exit to Brooklyn*, the Reverend David Sheppard was reported as saying that the book had not increased his understanding of people. He agreed that it was true, but it did not represent all the truth. Finally he said: 'I'm afraid it was pandering to all the worst in me and I would have to say that I'm not unscathed by reading a book like this.'[18] One might feel that on the evidence of Mr Sheppard's own words this book had succeeded in doing something that all literature sets out to do, which is to tell us something not only about other people, but also about ourselves. I would say that we are not meant to get through this world unscathed; rather we are meant to feel the depth and the degradation and the horror of it, and to know that these forces are in ourselves as well, in order that we may know how much compassion we ourselves need both to offer and to receive. Without wishing to cast any doubts on Mr Sheppard's integrity, I would suggest that his evidence tells in favour of the book, rather than against it.

Self-knowledge and openness to reality are not always a very strong suit with those who profess the Christian faith. In Britain, protests against obscenity, violence and blasphemy are a speciality of the National Viewers' and Listeners' Association (a body which includes among its supporters a number of clergy and at least one bishop). One of their protests was reported as follows:

LAW THREAT ON ALF GARNETT

Letters have been sent to Lord Hill, chairman of the BBC, and to the Primate of Australia, by the National Viewers' and Listeners' Association, which claims more than a million members, concerning Friday night's TV episode of 'Till Death Us Do Part'. This series is now being screened in Australia.

Mrs Mary Whitehouse, general secretary of the Association, has told the Archbishop that it 'completely dissociates' itself from the episode. She added: 'We are ashamed and angry that any part of our money should have been used in making this programme for transmission in Britain, let alone for export.'

The Association is asking Sir Norman Skelhorn, QC, Director of Public Prosecutions, to investigate if there are grounds for action against the BBC for transmitting what she calls 'blasphemous statements and comment'.

Mrs Whitehouse said yesterday the Association objected specifically to a remark about 'your bloody God' and to 'that rubbish, the Bible'.

'The whole weight of the programme was on one side, with the two youngsters contemptuous of God. The sum total was 100 per cent against the idea of God.

'This does not matter to older people but it is very bad for youngsters trying to establish their thinking.'

Lord Hill is also hearing from Lady Jane Birdwood, chairman of the London branch of the Association, about 'blasphemy and filth'. She is telling him that though members may be called cranks they may yet be 'the undertakers of the BBC'.[19]

It is curious that those who profess to speak in the name of Jesus of Nazareth should be so aggressive in defence of their beliefs, when this aggression is so precisely contrary to the teaching of that same Jesus about love and about forgiveness. 'How blest you are when you suffer insults and persecution and every kind of calumny for my sake.' The National Viewers' and Listeners' Association does not seem very conscious of being the recipient of a blessing in this respect, neither does it seem to have much idea of loving its enemies.

The link up of aggression, of moral violence, with sexual feeling may perhaps be detected in the use of the phrase, 'blasphemy and filth'. In the development of the personality, sexual excitation has an anal phase which precedes the genital phase, and anal activities thereafter retain some sexual interest.[20] It is interesting to note in this connection that Mr Enoch Powell, who seems to have deep fears about the mixing of black and white races, referred in one of his speeches to the alleged posting of excrement through a letter box, a point that is not of much value concerning the mixing of races (since it is the sort of action a disturbed person of any race might commit), but one that is rich in

109

sexual implications. The connection between 'blasphemy' and 'filth' (and also between blasphemy and money, which is another image for love/excrement) may have its origin for some people in the use of religious feelings as a front for sexual feelings, so that, for example, the sexual interest becomes centred on an idealized 'Man', Jesus, or an idealized 'Father', God, or an idealized 'Woman', Mary. This would help to explain why the emotional defence mechanisms which are called into play against 'blasphemy' and 'filth' are not amenable to correction by the teaching to suffer persecution gladly and to love your enemies: they relate not so much to the valid religious belief as to the underlying sexual needs for which, at that point, the religious material has become a cover.

One thing that is noticeable in this report is the failure to recognize that the figure of Alf Garnett (the leading character in 'Till Death Us Do Part') is intended as an exposure and criticism of the sentiments expressed rather than as an endorsement of them – is this perhaps part of a general inability to distinguish reality from fantasy which is implied by the lack of a sense of humour or irony? Certainly the concern for 'youngsters' to be protected, presumably against realizing that in real life there are people who are '100 per cent against the idea of God' suggests some wish to steer clear of reality.

In this chapter we have taken a selection of news items concerning some actions of society and examined them to see what is their real moral quality, and what are some of their possible underlying motivations. In the light of what the Sermon on the Mount says about love, I would suggest that the moral quality of our society does not look very good. The examples discussed here, which are taken mainly from British public life, may not be altogether representa-

110

tive of the moral state of western society, but at least they are real. The point of the experiment is that it should be carried out by all of us, constantly, so that we can make our moral decisions on the real world, and not on the world as it would like to present itself to us. I think that there is enough in this chapter to warrant the conclusion that a certain degree of moral violence, of lack of concern for the real interests of people, of insecurity and of sexual pressure underlies at least some of the professed moral attitudes and public actions of organized society.

This leads us to the general conclusion that perhaps the moral standards of society are always and necessarily too low. It may be that society is not capable of rising to those heights of concern for the individual that the Sermon on the Mount sets before us. For 'society' is a collection of people, ourselves, who have many different moral ideas and many different moral experiences. What emerges from this collection will usually be at best compromise and at worst hypocrisy. In this situation the function of the law is really limited to providing a framework of order within which we can live our lives. It is not the function of the law to enforce upon us moral ways of behaving, first of all, because the law does not know what these should be; secondly, because action which is compelled by the fear of punishment is not moral action; thirdly, because all compulsion is, at least potentially, violence. The demand of the Christian religion is that human beings should be given the chance to grow morally at their own pace and in their own way, making their own choices and this demand is in a sense a demand for revolution. It is, I think, the same demand that Stokely Carmichael put like this:

> Now the trouble with the West is that it feels it has the right to *give* everybody their independence. That's totally absurd. You can never *give* anyone their independence. All men are

111

born free. They are enslaved by other men. So that the only act that the men who enslaved them can do is, not give them their independence, but stop oppressing them. There's a very important difference, and I don't think people make that distinction all the time. I'm amazed when I pick up the paper and read that 'England today decided to give independence to the West Indies'. Who the hell is England to give me my independence? All they can do is stop oppressing me, get off my back. But it sounds so much nicer when they say, 'We're giving you your independence. You're ready for it now.' Rather than for them to admit to themselves: 'We're going to stop oppressing you because we're becoming a little bit more civilized; or because you're making it uncomfortable for us and we can no longer afford to oppress you at the price that you're asking us to pay.' Which is correct. But you wouldn't expect self-condemnation.[21]

'Get off my back' is a demand that is not easily understood by organized society, but it is the first move in putting the Sermon on the Mount into operation. That, perhaps, is why it is not put into operation very often.

NOTES

1. From a report in *The Guardian*, 30 January 1969, p. 6.

2. For example, Richard Hensman in *New Christian*, 6 February 1969.

3. *The Guardian*, 6 February 1968, p. 3.

4. *The Listener*, 20 February 1969, p. 236.

5. *The Guardian*, 28 January 1969, p. 4.

6. 24 January 1969, p. 22.

7. 9 January 1969, p. 9.

8. *The Guardian*, 12 February 1969, p. 4.

9. Peter Gladstone Smith in the *Sunday Telegraph*, 14 July 1968, p. 1.

10. 20 July 1968, p. 47.

11. John Ezard in *The Guardian*, 25 January 1968, p. 4.

12. *The Times,* 3 July 1968, p. 11.

13. Ian Wright, 23 January 1969, p. 3.

14. See, for example, Gerald Gardiner, QC, *Capital Punishment as a Deterrent: and the Alternative* (Gollancz, London, 1956); Sir Walter Moberly, *The Ethics of Punishment* (Faber & Faber, London, 1968).

15. *The Effectiveness of Punishment and Other Measures of Treatment* (Council of Europe, Strasbourg, 1967), p. 81.

16. *The Guardian*, 20 February 1969, p. 6.

17. *The Guardian*, 6 February 1969, p. 5.

18. *The Guardian*, 22 November 1967, p. 6.

19. *Sunday Telegraph*, 18 February 1968, p. 3.

20. See, for example, D. W. Winnicott, *The Child, the Family and the Outside World*, pp. 40–44.

21. 'Black Power', in *The Dialectics of Liberation* (Penguin, London, 1968), pp. 158 f.

7   What *Is* Right?

Go, said the bird, for the leaves were full of children,
Hidden excitedly, containing laughter.
Go, go, go, said the bird: human kind
Cannot bear very much reality.

T. S. Eliot, *Burnt Norton*

Human kind cannot bear very much reality. At every point
in this discussion we have come up against the gap between
what we believe about life and how life actually is. All our
talk about policy in Vietnam does not match the reality of
one child burned by napalm; our reaction to drug use is a
reaction more to fantasy than to fact; our reaction to
obscenity and blasphemy is largely a reaction to our own
fears. In short, our difficulties in loving are largely an extension of our difficulties in loving ourselves. We cut ourselves off from reality because we fear our own ability to
cope with it. The purpose of religious revelation – at any
rate, of the Christian revelation, for I cannot claim to
speak for any other – is to help us to see the reality which
underlies our own being and the being of others. The
Sermon on the Mount is an attempt to face us with the
necessity of love without limit. This love is possible to the
people that we are only because it begins not, 'You must
love', but 'God loves you'. This is the burning reality which
underlies our own lives and all life.

If this is the Christian ethic, it may raise two objections. The first is that we may not be able to live like this. Although most of the moral judgments we make in daily life are quite simple and can be made according to a rule, such as 'tell the truth', 'keep your promises', or 'give to the poor', situations arise in which we do not know how the rules apply, or when we wonder if the rules are really true. Then we are in deep waters. Two choices are open to us: to do what is conventional, or to allow ourselves to become aware of deeper demands and more exciting and more painful possibilities. God asks that we should act 'as we would if we loved this person', which is asking a lot. But he does not ask us to do this by ourselves: he invites us to join with him in doing it, and in so far as we fall short he makes up the difference for us. To us, enclosed in our own small space, he says, 'Come out of that; I love you; you can love others'. And we shall never know whether it is possible or not unless we try.

So here we come to the second obstacle: does God really say this? Is he not a God of judgment as well as of love? Have we not overstressed his love at the expense of his justice? Perhaps we have, but there are two things that we can say in our defence. The first is that the New Testament is quite clear in its insistence that for us to judge whether other people are guilty in God's sight is itself a sin, so that we may safely leave the question aside as not ours to settle. The other is that the insistence on the unselective love of God in the New Testament is so strong that it is difficult to hold it alongside the idea of God as a punishing God. Personally, I think that the New Testament warnings about judgment amount to a statement that we live in a moral world in the sense that hurtful actions are bound to bring hurtful results. The pain of the hurt that we have given cannot be avoided and the pain that we cause we will also feel and understand. John Hick in *Evil and the God of Love*[1] argues that this is a situation that is necessary to the process of moral growth, and that seems to me to be right. But final damnation does not square with a God of love.

Does this not sit rather lightly to some of what the Bible says? Perhaps it does. The Bible is not a final, clear, and exhaustive description of God: nothing that can be grasped by human minds could be that. The Bible is a sufficient description, in the sense that it is enough for us to work by, but it is also a profoundly human document that needs to be worked on by the human understanding in each age.

> The New Testament Christians were not men who had a full understanding of what Christianity is to which we must get back. They were men who, seeing things with the eyes of their time and place, took the first steps in trying to grasp the significance of the revelation of God in Christ, a process which has been going on ever since, in which we are still engaged.[2]

So we are faced with the choice, either of a rigid, punitive, and in the end inconsistent God (who is to be found in the Bible), or of a God who is love, freedom and reality (who is also to be found in the Bible). It is this latter God that Jesus and Paul know and put before us, not always consistently, but always with a certitude in the priority of these qualities. It is this God who is the answer to the question, 'What is right?' There is a long tradition in Christian and Jewish thought of sin as a revolt against God. Modern psychological knowledge suggests that sin is much more a revolt against ourselves and that 'guilt' is our unwillingness to accept and trust ourselves. The Christian Gospel is that we do not need to carry this load of guilt, because God loves us. It is a message of release, and part of the understanding of this release is to see that in a sense we *cannot* sin against God, because all our 'sin' is only a childish raging which no more changes God's love for us than the rage of a child changes the love of its parents. I do not mean to deny that we can really hurt each other, or that the hurt that is in the world is anything other than horrible and damaging (no one who has lived in this century of Belsen and Hiroshima could think otherwise), but I think finally that it is incompatible with what the Bible tells us of the *love* of God to say that he will ever cut us off from his love. God offers us the chance to be ourselves, to be sons, not slaves, and to be a son means to take the risk of being wrong, but in the confidence of God's ultimate love for us. It is a process that is not without pain, not without doubt and not without discouragement. But I think that it is a way of living that is in the long run more coherent and much happier than any other that is offered to us.

It is also, inevitably, a political way of life. Christianity is about love, and love is expressed in the kind of life we lead. We cannot try to act in love for very long before we come up against what society is actually doing. It is a denial of God to say that religion ought to keep out of politics. Christianity became political the day that Jesus went up to Jerusalem to carry his challenge about the quality of life into the heart of the power structure and to die a political death in the name of love. It has been necessary ever since for those who care about love to carry on the same challenge. The Christian who takes his religion seriously is going to be a disturber of the peace. It is not a pursuit that is going to make anyone very popular, but this is something that we just have to put up with. After all, it is the fate of anyone who asks seriously the question, 'What is right?'

NOTES

1. Fontana, London, 1969.
2. Leonard Hodgson, *Sex and Christian Freedom*, pp. 78 f.

For Further Reading

Leonard Hodgson, *Sex and Christian Freedom: An Enquiry* (London: SCM Press and New York: Seabury Press).

Douglas Rhymes, *No New Morality* (London: Constable). *Two brief but important discussions of sexuality and personal relationships.*

Joseph Fletcher, *Situation Ethics* (London: SCM Press, and Philadelphia: Westminster Press). *The book which broke new ground in trying to establish 'Act in love' as the ground of morality.*

Michael Keeling, *Morals in a Free Society* (London: SCM Press, and New York: Seabury Press). *Applies the principles discussed in the present book to a number of contemporary moral problems in British society.*

Lindsay Dewar, *An Outline of Anglican Moral Theology* (London: Mowbray). *An evaluation of the Anglican moral tradition from Hooker to Kirk.*

Antony Flew, *God and Philosophy* (London: Hutchinson). *A lucid demonstration of a philosopher's view of the inadequacy of the proofs for the existence of God and of the Natural Law.*

John Hick, *Evil and the God of Love* (London: Macmillan and Fontana, and New York: Harper & Row). *A discussion of the two basic approaches in theology to the* problem of evil, coming down on the side of a God of love rather than of punishment.

Erich Fromm, *The Fear of Freedom* (London: Routledge and Kegan Paul). *A psychologist's view of the reasons why we tend to prefer authoritarianism to the openness of love, first published in 1942 and still essential reading for anyone who either exercises authority or suffers from it.*

Harvey Cox, *The Secular City* (London: SCM Press and Penguin, and New York: The Macmillan Co.). *Theology welcoming the arrival of urban, secular, technological man: full of provoking thoughts.*

British Council of Churches, *World Poverty and British Responsibility* (London: SCM Press). *Plain statement of the needs of developing countries and the implications for Christian ethics; includes the text of the Encyclical* Populorum Progressio.

David Cooper (editor), *The Dialectics of Liberation* (London: Penguin Books). *Statements on the need for revolution made by a variety of speakers at the Roundhouse, London, in July 1967: connects with most of the larger social problems we face.*

Norman Mailer, *Miami and the Siege of Chicago* (London: Penguin Books). *Superbly written reports on the Republican and Democratic Party Conventions in 1968, conveying some of the feel of politics and violence in the USA.*

INDEX

Index

Interest wise facts an aid to under developed countries,
and the income such aid has given to the western
nation giving the aid.   66.